# USING LEARNING CENTERS WITH NOT-YET READERS

## An Aid For Abecedarians

This book is part of the Goodyear Education Series, Theodore W. Hipple, Editor, University of Florida.

## OTHER GOODYEAR BOOKS IN GENERAL METHODS AND CENTERS

**AH-HAH! The Inquiry Process of Generating and Testing Knowledge**
John McCollum

**A CALENDAR OF HOME/SCHOOL ACTIVITIES**
JoAnne Patricia Brosnahan and Barbara Walters Milne

**CHANGE FOR CHILDREN Ideas and Activities for Individualizing Learning**
Sandra N. Kaplan, Jo Ann B. Kaplan, Sheila K. Madsen, Bette K. Taylor

**CREATING A LEARNING ENVIRONMENT A Learning Center Handbook**
Ethel Breyfogle, Susan Nelson, Carol Pitts, Pamela Santich

**THE LEARNING CENTER BOOK An Integrated Approach**
Tom Davidson, Phyllis Fountain, Rachel Grogan, Verl Short, Judy Steely, Katherine Freeman

**ONE AT A TIME ALL AT ONCE The Creative Teacher's Guide to Individualized Instruction Without Anarchy**
Jack E. Blackburn and W. Conrad Powell

**OPEN SESAME A Primer in Open Education**
Evelyn M. Carswell and Darrell L. Roubinek

**THE OTHER SIDE OF THE REPORT CARD A How-to-Do-It Program for Affective Education**
Larry Chase

**THE TEACHER'S CHOICE**
Sandra N. Kaplan, Sheila K. Madsen, Bette T. Gould

**TEACHING FOR LEARNING Applying Educational Psychology in the Classroom**
Myron H. Dembo

**OTHER WAYS, OTHER MEANS Altered Awareness Activities for Receptive Learning**
Alton Harrison and Diann Musial

**WILL THE REAL TEACHER PLEASE STAND UP? A Primer in Humanistic Education, 2nd edition**
Mary Greer and Bonnie Rubinstein

**A YOUNG CHILD EXPERIENCES Activities for Teaching and Learning**
Sandra N. Kaplan, Jo Ann B. Kaplan, Sheila K. Madsen, Bette T. Gould

For information about these, or Goodyear books in Language Arts, Reading, Science, Math, or Social Studies, write to:

Janet Jackson
Goodyear Publishing Company
1640 Fifth Street
Santa Monica, CA 90401
(213) 393-6731

# USING LEARNING CENTERS WITH NOT-YET READERS
## An Aid For Abecedarians

TOM AND JUDY DAVIDSON AND STEELY

GOODYEAR PUBLISHING COMPANY, INC.
SANTA MONICA, CA

Library of Congress Cataloging in
Publication Data

Davidson, Tom, 1941-
    Using learning centers with not-yet readers.

    (Goodyear education series)
    1. Reading readiness.    2. Instructional materials
centers.    I. Steely, Judy, joint author.    II. Title.
LB1525.D38        372.4'142        77-20781
ISBN 0-87620-937-1
ISBN 0-87620-936-3 pbk.

Y-9363-6 (paper)
  9371-9 (case)

Current Printing (last number):
10 9 8 7 6 5 4 3 2 1

Printed in the United States of America

Text and Cover Design: Louis Neiheisel
Illustrations: Tom Davidson

# DEDICATION

This book is dedicated to those disappointed kids who haven't had the chance to work in centers because they can't read and understand directions and to those discouraged teachers who want to use centers with their Not-Yet Readers but who have sunk beneath a sea of problems. Our goal is to translate what has seemed impossible into a reality in these classrooms. We also dedicate this book to any other kids and teachers who can use our ideas to further self-directed learning in their classrooms, with a special dedication for Judy and Mel

Kathi
Karen
Sylvia
Jackie
Bonnie
Craig
Bernie
Foots
Sam
Wilbur

# 1. INTRODUCTION: SPOTLIGHT ON LEARNING CENTERS

If you are using learning centers now, have tried them before, or are just tending toward that direction, you may encounter one seemingly insurmountable problem. It goes something like this: Most of the kids will adapt themselves to centers, once they are accustomed to working on their own, reading directions, and staying on task. Why? **They READ!** But not all of your kids can read well enough to pick up directions and work on their own. If you teach kindergarten or early first-year children it may be that **none** of the kids reads well enough to do these things. Sound familiar? We empathize (we do!) with your plight. The simple fact is that unless kids can grasp directions and procedures for working in center activities, they won't know what to do, how they are to do it, or when or where they are supposed to do it. Right on target? We believe in calling our shots.

So what do you do? Do you give up on centers altogether? Do you give only the good readers the opportunity to work in centers? Do you spend hours giving oral directions to the kids who are poor readers so that they can have center experiences? Just what **do** you do?

Our classroom experience has proven that feasible alternatives to these choices exist. What do you say to practical ideas for learning center directions and management that do not require that kids be able to read? We think that these ideas will work as well for you as they have for us and for other teachers we have worked with. Interested? If you are, read on.

**LEARNING CENTERS: A CAPSULE LOOK**

During the past few years, the concept of learning centers has come under the scrutiny of the educational eye. It is not our purpose in this section to restate or rehash the literature on learning centers. We will discuss briefly here how to plan and use centers for maximum success, whether with not-yet readers or all kids. If the concept of learning centers is new to you, we recommend that you get into some of the sources listed at the end of this chapter.

There are several key elements in the concept of learning centers that we, and others, have found to be most pivotal to success.

1. Learning centers are what they imply, namely, centers in the classroom (or pod or area) that are designed to promote the mastery of skills, the acquisition of knowledge, the development of concepts, or the formation of generalizations. They are different from interest centers, exploratory centers, or game centers in that they are planned, organized, and developed around the identified learning needs of a specific group of children.

2. Learning centers may take on different guises, depending on the purpose for which they are designed. A center for math skills will have a setup assuredly different from that of a center geared to generalizations for an entire science unit. The form that a center should take is the one that best fits its purpose.

3. Learning centers require (PAY ATTENTION! The center you save may be your own) more organization, more structure, and more planning than any other form of instruction. You will avoid organized confusion and supervised chaos only to the extent that you carefully develop the underlying management structure of working in centers with the children, organize the materials and activities in the center, and plan center activities around the needs and interests of the kids who will be using them. While this all sounds like so much work and effort, the justification (and satisfaction) lies in the payoff. For a discussion of this, see the next section, Hidden Outcomes.

4. Learning centers are but one of several effective forms of instruction. Overuse of learning centers can be too much of a good thing. A variety of instructional techniques (packets, contracts, small and large groups)

used in conjunction with centers will keep instruction alive and well and kids' enthusiasm high.

Many other factors can, and will, influence your success with centers, but these four seem to be basic to the effectiveness of learning centers in the classroom. Taking these elements to heart, you will be able to use learning centers to help your students grow and learn.

Educators have made much ado about the amount of interest, motivation, and joy in learning stemming from the use of learning centers in the classroom. Excessive concern about these results has almost buried other important outcomes. It is vital that you, the classroom teacher, bring these hidden outcomes out in the open and keep them before you as you implement learning centers with your children.

## FREEDOM
A major outcome of learning centers that you should, and must, work toward is the creation of a **free learning atmosphere** for children. By **free**, we mean that it allows students to move around in the learning environment without fear of being told to sit down, to be quiet, to not talk or interact with others, or to not use materials. What we must recognize is that, especially for younger children (four- to thirteen-year-olds), movement and interaction are **natural developmental** tendencies that children must and will express as they function normally in their world, which includes school. Rather than attempting to stifle these natural manifestations, we must capitalize on them and help children learn how to fit these behaviors into a variety of situations — from quiet to noisy — and how to choose when to be quiet and when to be not-so-quiet. You must help children to learn how to function responsibly in a free environment, just as they learn to add or subtract or spell. And learning centers are a free environment.

## RESPONSIBILITY
A second major outcome of learning centers that you must work toward with children is the development of responsibility — responsibility for oneself and to others. This "for and to" distinction is a crucial one. First, you must help children to realize that they, and no one else, govern what they do and how they behave. In other words, they are in control of themselves. They are thus responsible for their own behavior in a social situation (the classroom, in this discussion) and can be held accountable for themselves. This is the **for** distinction.

Second, you must help children recognize that they are also responsible to others in a social situation (the classroom) to the extent that their behavior, which they are responsible for, may influence or infringe upon the rights of the others they are in contact with. With your guidance the children, as they function within a free environment, will recognize that their ability to be responsible **for** themselves has a direct bearing on those around them, **to** whom they are responsible. Learning centers, if they are to bring children to their full potential for learning, will offer the opportunity for you to work with your children to help them learn responsibility.

**SELF-DIRECTION**
A third and, for the purposes of this discussion, final hidden outcome of learning centers is the development of self-directed learners. The educational system of our nation professes one goal of education to be the development of citizens who can make decisions about their, and the nation's, future. However, we find it difficult, and seem to have always found it so, to go about doing this seriously.

The involvement of children in learning centers is one path to motivation. As children experience opportunities to make choices about their learning, to try out different ways of going about learning, to locate and organize their own learning materials, and to answer to the teacher for all of these things, they will be learning self-direction through concrete experience.

Children cannot absorb self-direction by osmosis. It must be learned by the self! So, as you introduce and extend the use of learning centers with your children, keep in mind that learning self-direction is as important to the children as their "other" learning.

The interest, motivation, and joy in learning that learning centers generate are only the "tip of the iceberg." The mass of the iceberg—the learning that will pay off next week, next year—is hidden below the surface. Successful learning center environments bring this mass—freedom, responsibility, and self-direction—up into the cold, clear light where it can be seen.

OK. We have now taken care of the general concern with learning centers. It's time to deal with the major topic of this book: the not-yet reader.

# SOURCES

Beech, Ronald W. **Reaching Teenagers.** Santa Monica, Ca.: Goodyear Publishing Co., 1977.

Blackburn, Jack E., and Powell, W. Conrad. **One At A Time All At Once.** Santa Monica, Ca.: Goodyear Publishing Co., 1976.

Breyfogle, Ethel; Nelson, Sue; Pitts, Carol; and Santich, Pamela. **Creating A Learning Environment.** Santa Monica, Ca.: Goodyear Publishing Co., 1977.

Davidson, Tom; Fountain, Phyllis; Grogan, Rachel; Short, Verl; Steely, Judy; and Freeman, Katherine. **The Learning Center Book.** Santa Monica, Ca.: Goodyear Publishing Co., 1976.

Forgan, Harry W. **The Reading Corner.** Santa Monica, Ca.: Goodyear Publishing Co., 1977.

Forte, Imogene, and MacKinzie, Joy. **Nooks, Crannies and Corners.** Nashville, Tenn.: Incentive Publications, 1971.

Kaplan, Sandra N.; Kaplan, Jo Ann B.; Madsen, Sheila K.; and Gould, Bette T. **A Young Child Experiences.** Santa Monica, Ca.: Goodyear Publishing Co., 1976.

Kaplan, Sandra N.; Kaplan, Jo Ann B.; Madsen, Sheila K.; and Taylor, Bette K. **Change For Children.** Santa Monica, Ca.: Goodyear Publishing Co., 1973.

Margrabe, Mary. **The "Now" Library Media Center.** Washington, D.C.: Acropolis Books, 1973.

Thomas, John I. **Learning Centers: Opening Up the Classrooms.** Boston: Holbrook Press, 1975.

Voight, Ralph Claude. **Invitation To Learning: Volume 1.** Washington, D.C.: Acropolis Books, 1971.

_____. **Invitation To Learning: Volume 2.** Washington, D.C.: Acropolis Books, 1975.

_____. **Invitation To Learning: Volume 3.** Washington, D.C.: Acropolis Books, 1976.

# 2. THE NOT-YET READER

This book and the ideas you will find in it are the outgrowth of a concern we share with most educators: the children we have chosen to call not-yet readers. We will now explain what we mean by not-yet readers, what some of the problems are for these children when they encounter learning centers, why we feel learning centers are a legitimate, necessary experience for not-yet readers, and what hidden outcomes surface when you use learning centers with not-yet readers.

# WHAT'S A NOT-YET READER?

The children we classify as not-yet readers in this book are of two basic types. First, there are children who because of their age (five- and six-year-olds) have **not yet** learned to read. They have had little or no formal reading instruction and, as a result, have very limited sight vocabulary (if any, other than "popular" words) and reading skill. This type of not-yet reader cannot handle directions or activities that require the reading of words. If presented continually with learning tasks that are reading based, these younger children are in danger of becoming not-yet readers of the second type.

The second group of children is those who because of a myriad of psychological, social, and emotional reasons, regardless of their age, have not yet learned to read. Oh, they may have had from one to eight years of formal reading instruction. But — the formidable array of preprimers, basal readers, workbooks, ditto sheets, and language experience and remedial programs directed at helping them learn to read notwithstanding — they have not been ready or motivated and just have **not yet** learned to read. Many of these children are turned off by and fearful of reading-oriented tasks, are not confident in their ability to become readers, cope with their fear and fatalism by misbehaving, and are too often doomed to a reading life that is dull and deadly. Their wider experience with reading instruction has not transported them beyond the level of the first group of not-yet readers. And this second type is a problem.

# PROBLEMS, PROBLEMS

It goes without saying (but we're going to say it anyway!) that attempting to implement learning centers with both young children and older children who are not-yet readers is a problem-studded task. And, because of the inherent problems, most of us have hesitated — if not refused — to try learning centers on for size with these children. Here we are to say to you that you can deal with these problems if you delve into their whats and whys. We can't go into all of the possible problems and their implications, but we can "raise your consciousness" to a few of the more significant ones.

The most obvious problem not-yet readers bring to the learning center environment is a lack of reading skill. In the preceding section we noted that this lack of reading skill could be the result of two other "lacks": a lack of formal reading instruction with younger children or — more serious — a lack of success in reading with older children. Whichever the case, consider this problem in the light of the reading requirement for a typical learning center. Directions about what to do and how to do it are usually printed. Learning centers present not-yet readers with a small-scale version of the same problem that most of school life entails: To be involved, successful learners they must read. And they can't. To involve these not-yet readers in learning centers, you must provide materials and activities and use techniques that sidestep the necessity of so much reading. You can do it if you begin to be sensitive and responsive to the problem.

A second problem not-yet readers bring to the learning center environment is their attitude toward learning — especially learning to read — in general, and toward themselves, as learners, in particular. Older children are more prone to this second problem. The failure-pressure-more failure cycle quickly turns off not-yet readers to any learning situation that ostensibly requires reading. Faced with fiasco in learning to read and with increased efforts and, too often, a geometric increase in pressure on the part of frustrated teachers, not-yet readers usually develop a very poor concept of their ability to be or become successful learners. The combination of an antipathy toward the school environment and a personal conviction of scholastic ineptitude creates one of the most solid barriers you will come up against in the classroom. And yet, to lower that barrier to learning, you must put forth the effort to get not-yet readers actively involved, successfully, with the learning environment.

Last, not-yet readers, like all human beings, develop ways of coping with the pressure of unsuccessful experiences. Alternative ways of behaving in the learning center environment emerge: fomenting chaos and confusion, not paying attention or staying on task, or daydreaming. These alternative behaviors are the result of not-yet readers' inability to accommodate the demands to read, follow directions, and complete reading-oriented tasks. To counter these things, you must deemphasize their inability to read and transform a handicap into a success in the learning center environment.

Another sore spot we would like to probe before getting to some specific planning how-to-do-its is the attitude that schools tend to convey to not-yet readers. This attitude demonstrates (we know, not always!) a lack of confidence, poor expectations, and the weary do-it-over-and-over-until-you-get-it-right mentality. Can you doubt its negative effect on not-yet readers?

First, if you treat children as if you have no confidence in their ability to be successful, they will probably prove you right. Once categorized, not-yet readers usually meet the lack of confidence on a daily basis both at school and at home. And they certainly respond to it. They **learn** one thing: They have no grounds for self-confidence.

Second, if you never expect these children to complete tasks, to master skills, or to function on their own, they will never (well, almost never) do so. Signed, sealed, and delivered, the not-yet reader experiences low expectations on a regular basis. We have all heard "Well, what can you expect from someone with reading scores like his?" over coffee or around the workroom at our schools. This attitude poisons the minds of not-yet readers. They **learn** that they needn't do much because very little is expected of them. So far we have indeed offered our not-yet readers learning experiences — negative ones.

Third, if you persist in giving children more and more of the same thing with which they have been unsuccessful in the past, they will not suddenly meet with success. The opposite effect is usually "achieved." Why, then, do not-yet readers have to experience more-of-the-same worksheets, workbook pages, kits, and drills over and over, day in and day out? All of which simply reinforce their failure; tell them that learning, and school in general, is dull, boring, and painful; and show them that everyone else gets to do all the fun stuff. And (you guessed it!), this third attitude removes not-yet readers even further from the learning scene. They eventually learn that the process of learning to read will always involve things that have little, if anything, to do with them.

You are probably aware by now that it is our feeling that not-yet readers need to enjoy dignity and respect, work with positive expectations, and have as many fun and exciting learning experiences as other children. This is the learning center experience. They need to be able to make choices in centers — with your guidance. They need to have tasks to complete — tasks they are **expected** to complete. They need to experience opportunities to be independent, to be responsible, and to be held accountable for their work. The not-yet readers in your classroom are people, too. They need to be treated as such, like everyone else.

# 3. GIVING DIRECTIONS TO NOT-YET READERS

How do you give learning center directions to not-yet readers? Verrry Slowllly. Move them from easy directions to more complicated ones. Begin by explaining orally how to use the directions. Then, when kids are accustomed to following center directions, they will need less teacher help. You can now institute written directions. Progress from directions that are mainly pictures and symbols to directions that use words.

The simplest directions for an activity or set of activities are oral explanations. Start kids off with activities and tasks using only oral directions. Remember that there is nothing for them to refer back to, so be sure that they are clear about what is expected. Keep the number of activities and/or tasks small; gradually introduce more activities into each new center.

# FROM LIP READING TO "SYMBOLIC LOGIC"

When your children are used to following directions in centers, muster up all your imagination and write the directions on poster paper using as many symbols and pictures in place of words as possible. Each time certain pictorial "words" appear, use the same symbol you have previously used so that kids will become familiar with the "language" and will understand more quickly. Review the meaning of the symbols periodically, being sure to show students the words the symbols stand for. These words will gradually become sight words that the children have mastered through constant use.

# For Example:

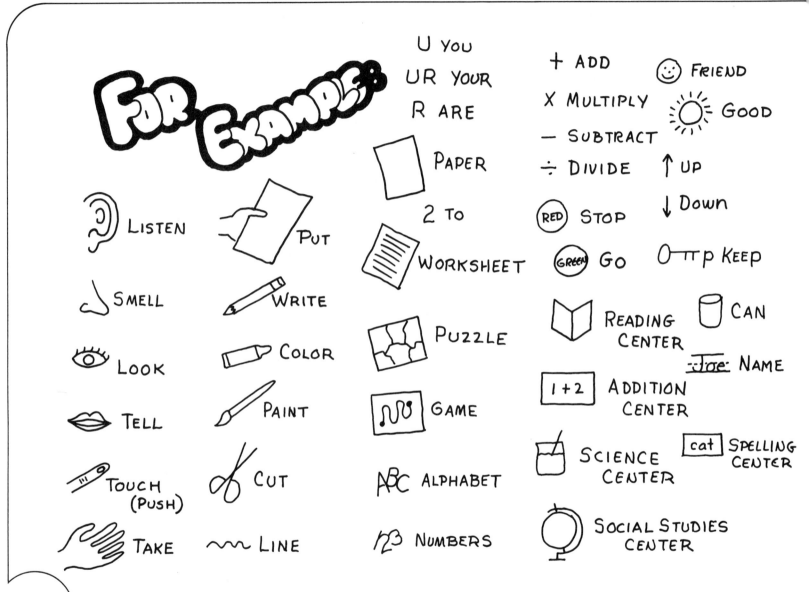

U you
UR your
R are

Paper

2 to

Worksheet

Listen

Put

Smell

Write

Look

Color

Tell

Paint

Touch
(Push)

Cut

Take

Line

Puzzle

Game

ABC Alphabet

123 Numbers

+ Add
x Multiply
− Subtract
÷ Divide

RED Stop
GREEN Go

☺ Friend
Good
↑ Up
↓ Down

Op Keep

Reading
Center

Can

Joe Name

1+2 Addition
Center

Science
Center

cat Spelling
Center

Social Studies
Center

Now you're ready to sneak a few words into your directions. These words will soon become sight vocabulary for your kids. Draw and write your directions on poster paper, using both pictures and words. When you introduce the center, point to each picture and word and read the directions to the children. As they work in the center they can refer back to the poster if they need further explanation or reminders. After a little practice at reading picture and word directions, children will remember the symbols you use so that each experience improves their direction-reading skills.

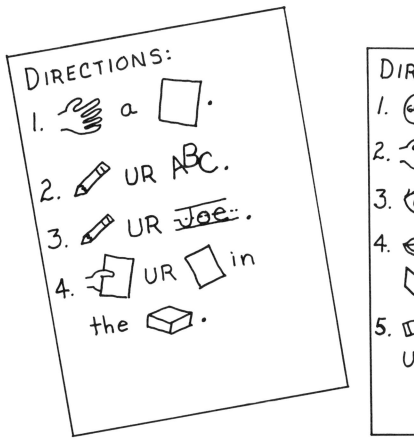

Every so often slip in a direction sheet that has many words and only a few pictures on it. Use words you know the children have become familiar with to assure their success at reading the directions.

DIRECTIONS:

1. Take a ▭.
2. ✎ your ABC.
3. ✐ your name.
4. Put your ▯ in the box.

DIRECTIONS:

1. Go to the 📖.
2. Take a book.
3. Look at your book.
4. Tell a ☺ about your book.
5. Color a 🏠 about your book.

WAIT JUST A MINUTE! Don't make directions on a plain old piece of poster paper every time. Make a catchy come-on! What's a catchy come-on? It might be a big cardboard or poster paper likeness of Big Bird saying, "Hey gang, come to my center!" Follow this with your directions written on a card and hung around Big Bird's neck. Or it might be a funny-looking rabbit, drawn on poster paper, saying, "I'm no dumb bunny! Look at this!" Then draw and write your directions on his droopy ears. You want more? Try painting or covering with contact paper an opened-out cardboard box and put-

- When finished, let me check your report.
- Share with two other people.

## DID YOU KNOW?

There are some very strange animals in the world today. Try these activities and find out.

1. Choose one of these animals:

   Platypus    Sloth      Gar

   Anteater   Mongoose

2. Write a one-page report about your animal. Tell:
   - Why it is strange.
   - What it eats.
   - What it looks like.

3. Draw a map to show where it lives.

4. Draw a picture of your animal.

ing your directions on white construction paper clouds all over the inside of the box. Stand it up in the center and kids will love it. Still more? Don't open out the box — paint it, then use the four sides to mount direction sheets. Get the idea? Here are more.

1. Take a ☐

2. ✏ UR ABC.

3. ✏ UR name.

WITCHES, GOBLINS, and SUCH!

EVER WONDER WHETHER THERE IS ANY BASIS FOR ALL THE SCARY STORIES ABOUT WITCHES, GHOSTS, AND GOBLINS?
TRY THIS!

ACTIVITY 1
A. Go to the library and see if there are any books about these things. Check one out.

B. Find one example of a FACTUAL event about these things.

To create interest in a science center on the planets, blow up large balloons to various sizes approximating the proportions of actual planets. Hang them from the ceiling in the center or across the room. Attach direction cards to a string and hang these from each "planet."

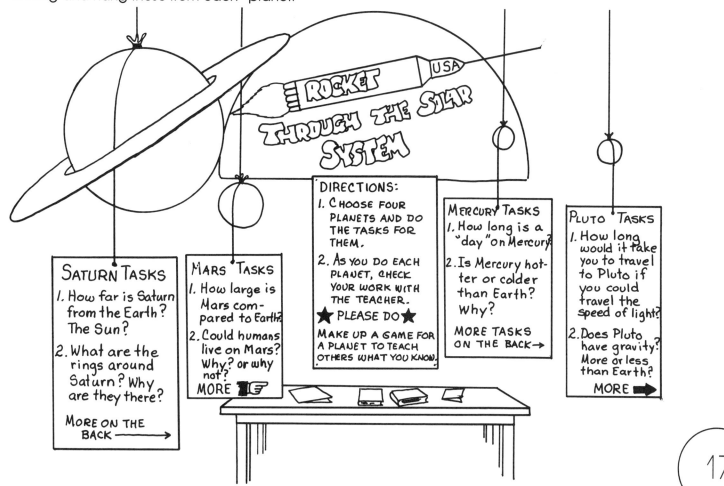

**ROCKET THROUGH THE SOLAR SYSTEM**

USA

DIRECTIONS:
1. CHOOSE FOUR PLANETS AND DO THE TASKS FOR THEM.
2. AS YOU DO EACH PLANET, CHECK YOUR WORK WITH THE TEACHER.
★ PLEASE DO ★
MAKE UP A GAME FOR A PLANET TO TEACH OTHERS WHAT YOU KNOW.

SATURN TASKS
1. How far is Saturn from the Earth? The Sun?
2. What are the rings around Saturn? Why are they there?

MORE ON THE BACK ———→

MARS TASKS
1. How large is Mars compared to Earth?
2. Could humans live on Mars? Why? or why not?

MORE 👉

MERCURY TASKS
1. How long is a "day" on Mercury?
2. Is Mercury hotter or colder than Earth? Why?

MORE TASKS ON THE BACK →

PLUTO TASKS
1. How long would it take you to travel to Pluto if you could travel the speed of light?
2. Does Pluto have gravity? More or less than Earth?

MORE ➡

To get kids interested in a math center on metric measurement, make a giant meter stick from poster paper. At each tenth centimeter, print the directions for an activity in the center.

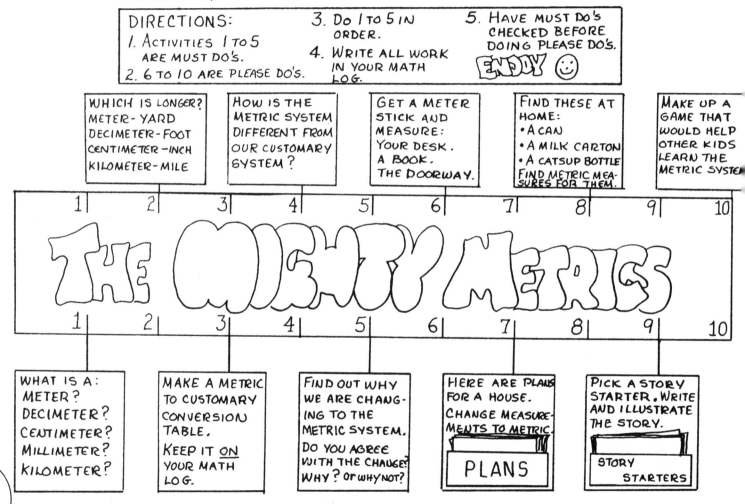

DIRECTIONS:
1. Activities 1 to 5 are must do's.
2. 6 to 10 are please do's.
3. Do 1 to 5 in order.
4. Write all work in your math log.
5. Have must do's checked before doing please do's.
ENJOY ☺

WHICH IS LONGER?
METER - YARD
DECIMETER - FOOT
CENTIMETER - INCH
KILOMETER - MILE

HOW IS THE METRIC SYSTEM DIFFERENT FROM OUR CUSTOMARY SYSTEM?

GET A METER STICK AND MEASURE:
YOUR DESK.
A BOOK.
THE DOORWAY.

FIND THESE AT HOME:
• A CAN
• A MILK CARTON
• A CATSUP BOTTLE
FIND METRIC MEASURES FOR THEM.

MAKE UP A GAME THAT WOULD HELP OTHER KIDS LEARN THE METRIC SYSTEM

THE MIGHTY METRICS

WHAT IS A:
METER?
DECIMETER?
CENTIMETER?
MILLIMETER?
KILOMETER?

MAKE A METRIC TO CUSTOMARY CONVERSION TABLE.
KEEP IT ON YOUR MATH LOG.

FIND OUT WHY WE ARE CHANGING TO THE METRIC SYSTEM.
DO YOU AGREE WITH THE CHANGE? WHY? OR WHY NOT?

HERE ARE PLANS FOR A HOUSE.
CHANGE MEASUREMENTS TO METRIC.
PLANS

PICK A STORY STARTER. WRITE AND ILLUSTRATE THE STORY.
STORY STARTERS

For a creative writing center on Halloween, pin or glue construction paper ghosts, witches, and other goblins to cork board, acoustical tile, or a piece of poster paper. On the chest of each spook write the directions for the activities at this center.

GHOSTLY TALES

DIRECTIONS
1. Choose an activity.
2. Illustrate and share.

STARTLING STARTERS
1. I swallowed the vile liquid and...
2. As I fell into the pit...
3. The horrible creature grabbed me and...

TERRIBLE TITLES
1. Eaten alive!
2. 100 spiders!
3. Slime!
4. The Coffin!

FREAKY'S FUN
Finish these stories.
THESE ARE HORRIBLE

Use a small stepladder as an invitation to any center. Put the title of the center on poster paper and affix it to the top of the ladder, then put directions on each descending step. You can also put the title at the bottom and challenge kids to work up the ladder of activities until they reach the stars at the top. Stars would be bonus activities, treats, or privileges.

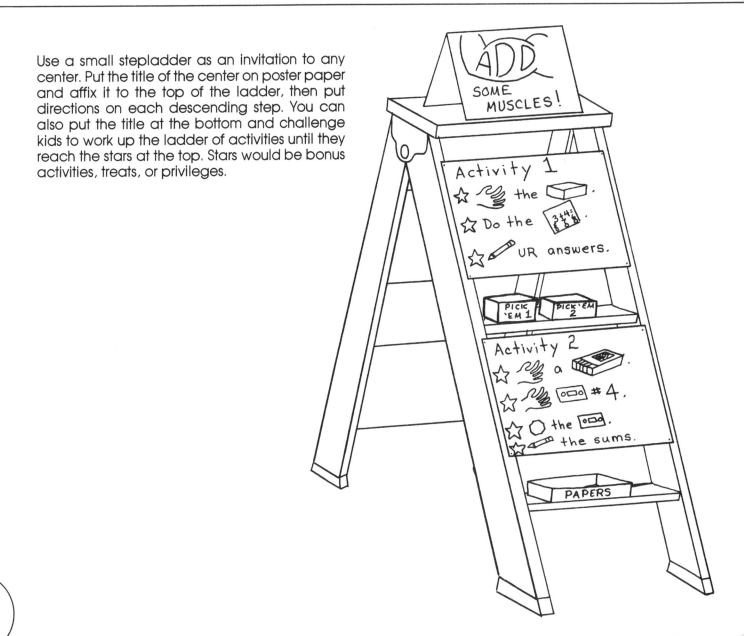

For a center on punctuation, paint a large box such as the kind a television, washer, or refrigerator comes in. Make giant punctuation marks and glue or tape them to the sides of the box. Put directions for activities about punctuation on these giant commas, question marks, exclamation points, and periods. Glue or tape a large manila envelope to each side of the box to hold worksheets or finished tasks.

A. What is this mark?

B. When should it be used?

C. Take one of these.

Look at the sentences.

Put a ? when it is needed.

PUT FINISHED PAPERS HERE

A. What mark is this?

B. Name three places where it might be used.

C. Read this story and decide where ,s are needed.

Write the story and put in the missing ,s.

D. Check work with the key.

KEY

A mobile can be an eye-catching enticement for any center. Put directions and explanations on the different pieces of the mobile, or hang manila envelopes from the mobile with task cards, puzzle pieces, or lace-up games inside.

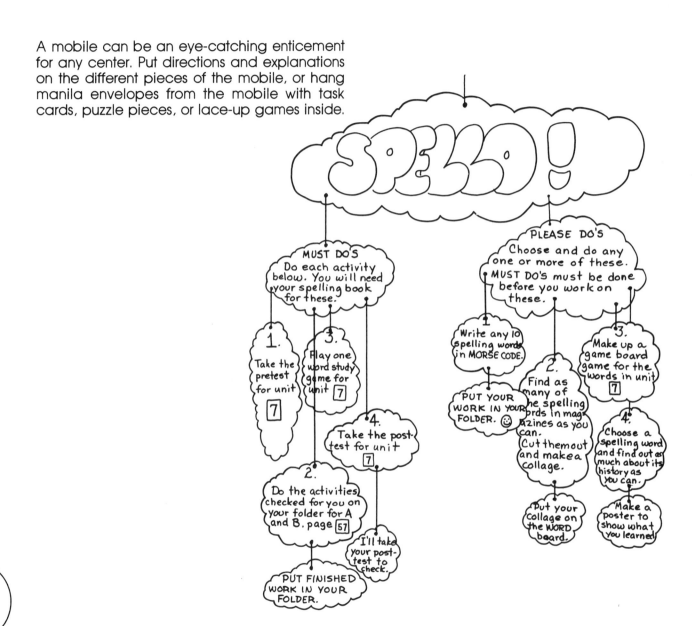

For a center on geometry, make large three-dimensional shapes such as a cube, prism, and octagon, and put directions for activities for each shape on its many sides.

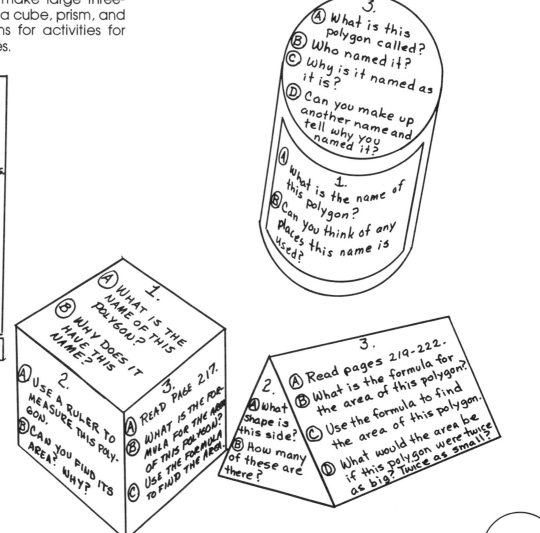

GEOMETRIC GEMS
DIRECTIONS:
1. Choose a Polygon.
2. Begin with activity 1 and complete all activities.
3. Record your work in you Math Log.
4. Choose another polygon.
5. Continue until you have done all three.
6. When done, turn in your log.

YOU WILL NEED YOUR MATH BOOK PAGES 215 TO 231 FOR THESE.

3.
Ⓐ What is this polygon called?
Ⓑ Who named it?
Ⓒ Why is it named as it is?
Ⓓ Can you make up another name and tell why you named it?

1.
Ⓐ What is the name of this polygon?
Ⓑ Can you think of any places this name is used?

1.
Ⓐ WHAT IS THE NAME OF THIS POLYGON?
Ⓑ WHY DOES IT HAVE THIS NAME?

2.
Ⓐ USE A RULER TO MEASURE THIS POLYGON.
Ⓑ CAN YOU FIND ITS AREA? WHY?

3.
READ PAGE 217.
Ⓐ WHAT IS THE FORMULA FOR THE AREA OF THIS POLYGON?
Ⓑ USE THE FORMULA TO FIND THE AREA.

2.
Ⓐ What shape is this side?
Ⓑ How many of these are there?

3.
Ⓐ Read pages 219-222.
Ⓑ What is the formula for the area of this polygon?
Ⓒ Use the formula to find the area of this polygon.
Ⓓ What would the area be if this polygon were twice as big? Twice as small?

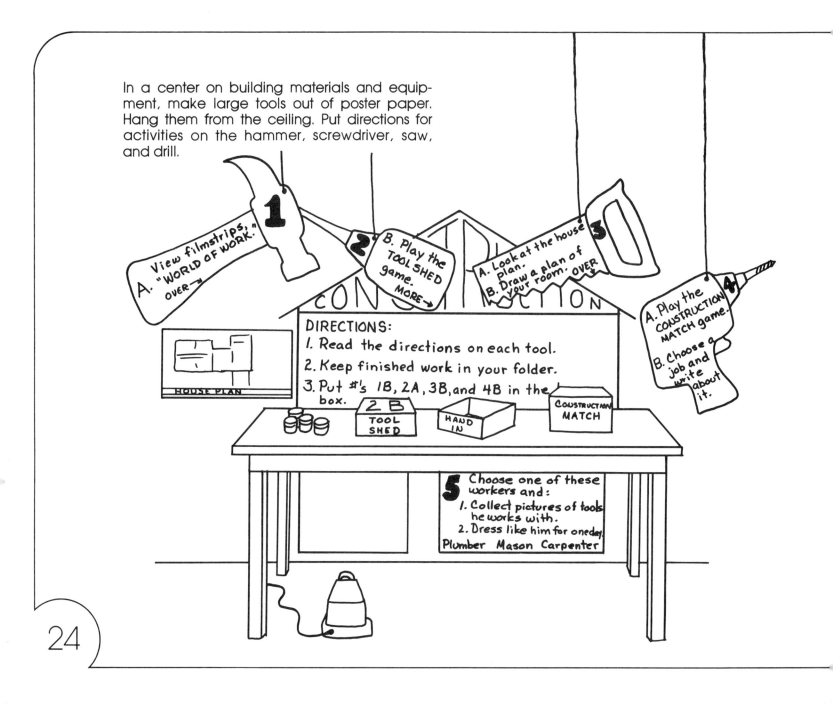

In a center on building materials and equipment, make large tools out of poster paper. Hang them from the ceiling. Put directions for activities on the hammer, screwdriver, saw, and drill.

**1** A. View filmstrips, "WORLD OF WORK." OVER →

**2** B. Play the TOOL SHED game. MORE →

**3** A. Look at the house plan. B. Draw a plan of your room. OVER

**4** A. Play the CONSTRUCTION MATCH game. B. Choose a job and write about it.

HOUSE PLAN

DIRECTIONS:
1. Read the directions on each tool.
2. Keep finished work in your folder.
3. Put #'s 1B, 2A, 3B, and 4B in the box.

2 B TOOL SHED

HAND IN

CONSTRUCTION MATCH

**5** Choose one of these workers and:
1. Collect pictures of tools he works with.
2. Dress like him for one day.

Plumber   Mason   Carpenter

**OTHER WAYS and MEANS**

No, no, no — drawing and writing directions and using catchy come-ons are NOT the only ways to give kids an explanation of the activities in a center. You can use a tape recorder to tell them their how-tos. Tape-record your directions on a cassette tape and place it in the center. Put a red mark on the stop button of the tape recorder, a green mark on the start button, and a smiley face on the rewind button. Explain to your children that they simply put the direction tape in the player, push the smiley button to get the tape to the beginning, push the green button, and sit back and listen. When the explanation is over, they push the red button to stop it and get busy on the chosen task. This method of receiving directions is fun for children and cuts through a lot of red tape!

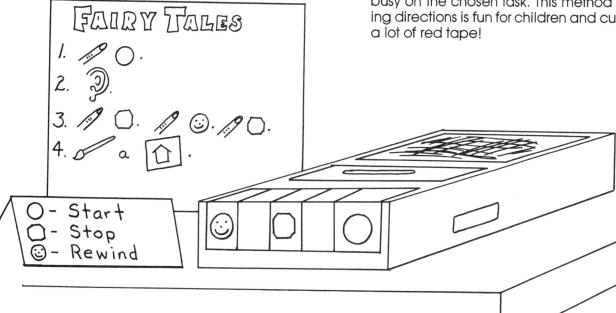

Another way to use the tape recorder in direction giving is to tape the directions and create a booklet to illustrate them. As your voice recites the directions, children turn the pages of your booklet and see a picture of the activity to accompany what they are hearing. It is easy for them to refer back to the booklet when they get stuck or forget something along the way. The booklet provides an opportunity for "getting-ready" readers to practice the reading skills they are developing.

ACTIVITY 3
A. Go to the library.
B. Find a book about Birds.
C. Pick one Bird.
D. Draw a picture of it.
E. Write two facts about it.

An effective and fun-to-use tool for taping directions is the Language Master. Tape-record your explanation of an activity or task on a Language Master card and file it in an activity box, envelope, or folder. Code it with colors, numbers, or letters so that children can put the card back with the appropriate activity when they have finished using it. When your kids get ready to do a task, they play the card on the Language Master and then do the activity. Simple — **if** you have a Language Master.

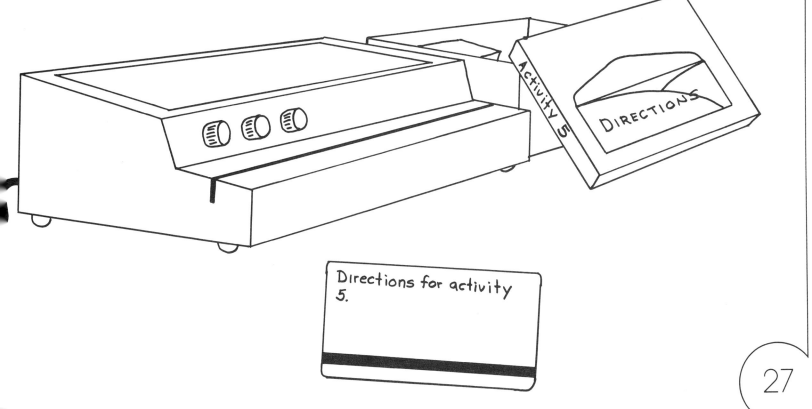

But that's not all; we have not yet exhausted the possibilities. You can use the buddy system to help kids understand directions. Pair up a child who can read fairly well with one who is a not-yet reader. The not-yet reader reads as much of the directions as possible. The buddy can help with the parts that lead the not-yet reader into the tangled underbrush. Another option is to let the buddy do all the reading; the not-yet reader can listen and learn. CAUTION: In using this system you must take into consideration who is friendly with whom in your classroom. Boys and girls may not take kindly to being paired with a member of the opposite sex, and then the expletives will fly: Boys, ughhhh! Girls, blahhhh! On the other hand, you might have more success putting that lovely young girl with. . . .

Here is another idea in direction giving. Many times you might ask the children to help plan a center, or you might ask them what activities they would like to do during a certain study. When you do this, make up an experience chart with them during the planning session to use for the directions for that center. Again, draw as many pictures in place of words as you feel are necessary for the children's clear understanding of what they are to do. Sometimes after a field trip or a class session, students can use an experience chart to recall what they have already learned and to plan activities for further learning on the subject. Having the children's own words and plans to work by is a great motivator in a center, and you have ready-made "experts" on the sentences that particular children have come up with.

Another way to keep kids on the right sequence if the activities are ordered (without getting path-ological about it) is to put directions in left-to-right order or top-to-bottom order. If you are one of those who like to wander off the straight and narrow, try making a path on the direction sheet. Draw and write your directions all along the path. Just be sure your kids start off on the right path. We wouldn't want any of them to get lost along the way, would we?

When you draw, tape, or write directions, number, color code, or letter the activities as a boon to yourself and your students. Children can follow the sequence of tasks by following the numbers, colors, or letters on the direction sheet. Yes, even colors can have a regular sequence if you always use red first, then yellow, blue, green, orange, purple, brown, black, pink, white, and so on. Post a color sequence chart in the room and leave it for children to refer to for the whole year. They will always know that the red activity is first, then yellow — a spectrum of ideas opens wide before them! If there's no sequence that the kids must follow in doing the activities in some centers, just think how much easier it will be for you and the kids to know which activities they have completed and which ones they still must finish. After they do each task they record it in some way by its letter, color, or number.

# 4.

# MANAGEMENT TECHNIQUES THAT WORK

How do kids know how many people can be in a center at one time? How do you know who's done what and when, and if they haven't? How do you get kids into centers? How do you get them from center to center? How do you keep things in order once they've started, other than by becoming a gavel pounder?

You've seen kids in centers who have the butterfly syndrome. They flit from center to center, never stopping at one for more than a few minutes, then off they go to another area. Sound familiar? You've got a FLITTERER on your hands. Read on.

31

Do you have children who just can't make up their minds about what center or project to choose? First they say they will and then they won't, now you see them, now you don't! Your problem is a not-so-rare species of the NON-CHOOSER, commonly known as the oh-teacher-I-just-can't-decide-what-to-doer. (Be forewarned: Your taxonomic task may turn into another **Origin of Species**.)

Have you noticed lurking in your centers kids who seem to be working until you discover them only half completing the tasks set up there? You've discovered the two-legged NON-FINISHER we all know and love. How do you deal with this species? Survival of the fittest?

There are some kids who seem to keep disappearing into centers that are not options for them at that particular time. These stealthy students are the GET-LOSTERS. Want to help them get found? Wait, don't get lost yet — there's more.

Have you ever noticed a center that looks like a beehive? Ten kids are falling all over each other because there's only enough room for four. These are your GATHERERS. They all fight for room like cars on a freeway at rush hour. What do you do about this "bumper" crop?

Do all these questions and situations echo in your brain? This phenomenon is quite normal. Almost everyone who starts using centers experiences it and **continues** experiencing it. Add not-yet readers to the kids who can read and the problem really gets complicated. We've gathered together some practical answers to your questions on the following pages. These ideas really do work, but don't take our word for it — try them and see.

To regulate how many kids can be at a center at a time, have tickets at the center. Children at the center must have a ticket. When the tickets are all gone they must wait until someone is finished and a ticket is available to go to the center. There is no such thing as "standing room only" with this method.

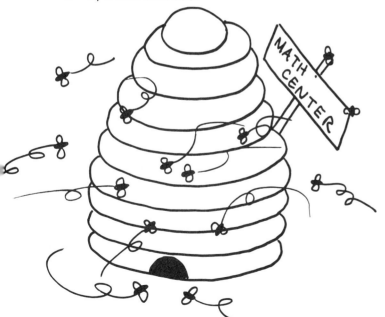

Take a ticket when you go into the center. Put it back when you leave.

Admit 1

TICKETS

If a center is limited to a certain number of persons, say four, put up four hooks and hang tags or badges for kids to wear from them. After deciding on the center, a child takes a tag or badge from the hook, puts it on, works in the center, then replaces it on the hook upon leaving the center. If a child wants to visit a center but there are no tags or badges available on the hooks, knowing that the center limit has been reached will prompt the child to make the decision to wait or to work in another area until someone leaves the center.

When you enter this center, take a necklace. Leave it when done.

## ACTIVITY 1

DIRECTIONS

1. Get five 🗂's.

2. Fill each 🗂 with some 〜.

3. Hit each 🗂 and 🎵.

4. Do they sound the same or different?

5. ✏ three sentences telling why.

6. Go to 🚶 two.

34

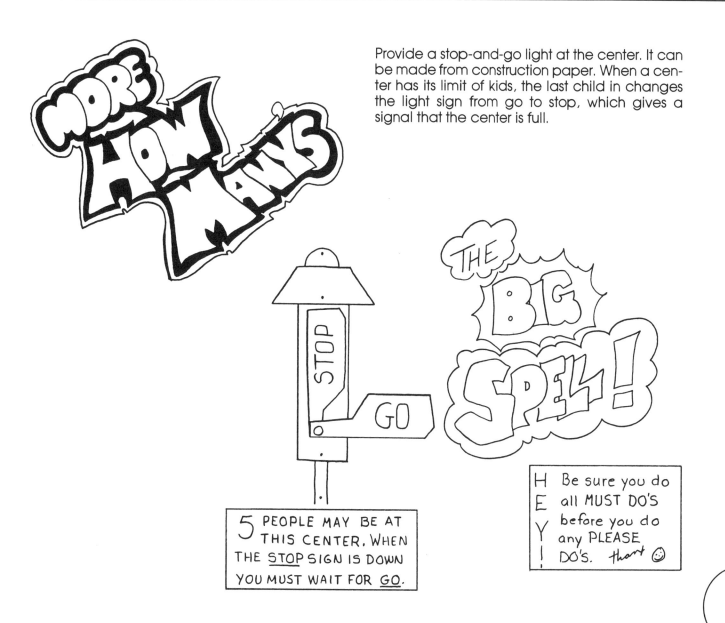

Provide a stop-and-go light at the center. It can be made from construction paper. When a center has its limit of kids, the last child in changes the light sign from go to stop, which gives a signal that the center is full.

5 PEOPLE MAY BE AT THIS CENTER. WHEN THE STOP SIGN IS DOWN YOU MUST WAIT FOR GO.

H Be sure you do
E all MUST DO'S
Y before you do
! any PLEASE
DO'S. thart ☺

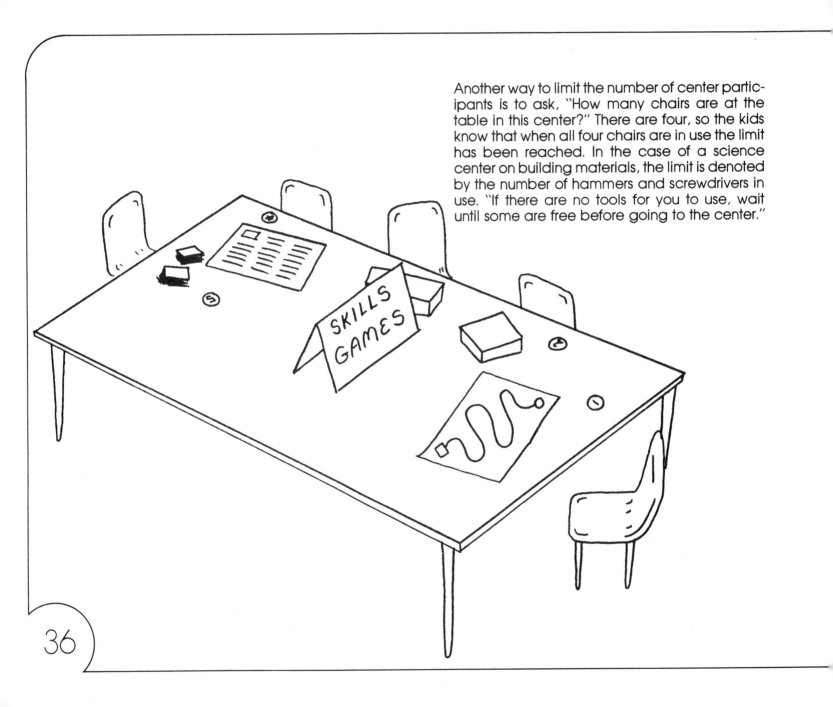

Another way to limit the number of center participants is to ask, "How many chairs are at the table in this center?" There are four, so the kids know that when all four chairs are in use the limit has been reached. In the case of a science center on building materials, the limit is denoted by the number of hammers and screwdrivers in use. "If there are no tools for you to use, wait until some are free before going to the center."

SKILLS GAMES

A key can also be used. When the keys are all gone for a center, the child knows that someone must leave and replace a key in a pocket before there is room at the center.

UNLOCK A TALE!

ONLY 4 persons may be at this center.

Take a key when you start.

If there are no keys, you must wait.

KEYS

## TASK 1

a. Go to the media center and find a book of TALL or FAIRY TALES.

b. Read several of the tales.

## TASK 2

a. Take one of these and answer the questions about tales.

Put completed work in this box. ⬇

## TASK 3

a. Write a TALL or FAIRY TALE of your own. Be sure to make it fit the rules for tales.

## TASK 4

a. Draw or paint a picture or set of pictures of the best part of your tale.

b. Put your work up on the TALES board.

Make a large pig out of poster paper. Make an ear of corn for each child, complete with name, and place it in the basket beside the pig. As the center is completed, the child "feeds" the corn to the pig by hanging it on a hook near the pig's mouth. You can adapt this concept to many other animals. Feed the horse an apple, the monkey a banana, the rabbit a carrot, and your centers will be stocked with contented animals — and students.

Feed The Pig!

Mr. Pig is very hungry for corn. When you have finished this center, write your name on an ear of corn and hang it so Mr. Pig can eat it.

To tell who has completed an activity, task, or entire center, provide a flower, bee, or some other symbol with a magnet attached to the back of it. When children fulfill requirements they take their magnetic symbols and stick them to a prescribed metal area (the side of a file cabinet or a metal sheet) in the room.

Make a large cardboard tree with a hook on it for each child. Place red construction paper apples with children's names on them in a basket at the base of the tree. As children finish activities, they draw worms coming out of their apples for each activity completed and place their wormy apples on the tree after they have finished all the activities. We have found that, on the "hole," kids enjoy using this method and don't try to worm their way out of working.

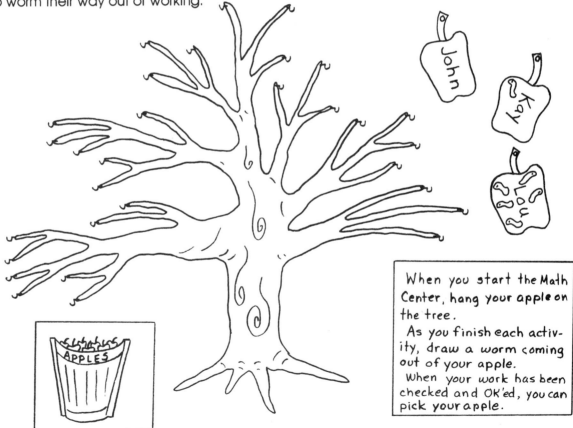

When you start the Math Center, hang your apple on the tree.

As you finish each activity, draw a worm coming out of your apple.

When your work has been checked and OK'ed, you can pick your apple.

Make tickets for the center with a symbol (numerals, letters, shapes, and so on) for each activity in the center. As kids finish each activity they punch a hole with a hole puncher beside the symbol for that activity. A finished ticket might be good for entrance to a fun center or a listening center. For example, present four tickets at the listening center for ten minutes of John Denver music. Use your imagination and you can come up with lots of variations on this theme (to carry over music to metaphor!).

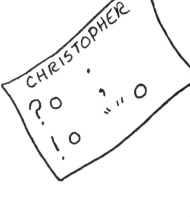

How do you feel about making your students into flower children? For each activity in a center or for each center set up for the day or week, make a flower petal that is color coded to the activity or center. When kids finish a task they take the flower petal for the completed activity and add it to a stem displayed somewhere in the room. They keep adding petals for activities until the center is completed and the flower has all its petals—then you can "leave" the blossomed flower as a room decoration.

All aboard the math train! Tape or pin a train engine to the wall or bulletin board. Provide a train car for each child with his or her name on it in the center or elsewhere in the room. As children complete their first activity in the center, they add their name cars to the train. Have children add something to their train cars, like a sticker or crayon symbol, every time they finish another activity in the center.

Another effective way to tell who's done what is to make a necklace or badge for use in the center. Big Bird necklaces made of construction paper and yarn, labeled with each child's name and a list of the activities at the center, are a good ploy. As they choose and complete tasks, children check off the items on the list. After all activities are completed, the necessary information can be transferred to a master chart or list for your records and the children can take their necklaces home. You can make a necklace as a symbol for any center or unit of study—a Liberty Bell necklace for a unit on America or an Indian head necklace for a study of native Americans, for example.

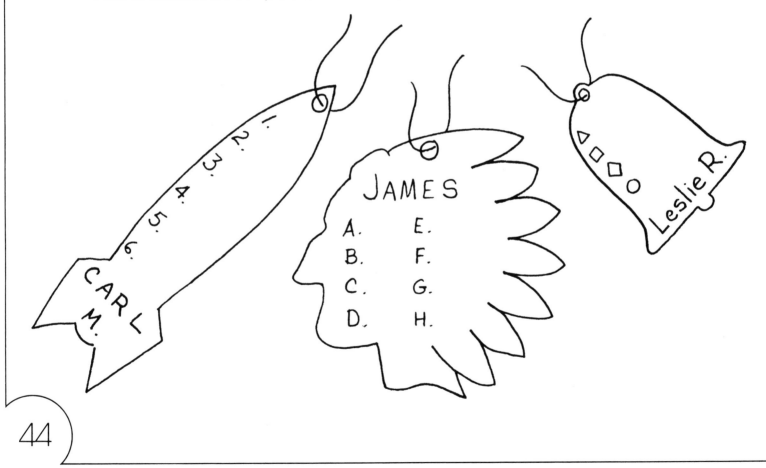

Some activities or centers might lend themselves to a conference with your kids to see how they are progressing. You can do this informally, using notes from your records, or you can use a formal check sheet. It is probably a good technique to use one of these types of interviews with kids so that you can get to know how they think and plan their use of time, and how they go about doing the activities.

In a center such as one on transportation, make a puzzle piece for each activity to be completed. Draw a car, bus, truck, airplane, and other types of transportation on pieces of construction paper. Cut each picture into as many pieces as there are activities at the center. Put one child's name on the back of all the pieces for one picture, then divide pieces for each picture into piles, with one piece for each child in each pile. Place each set of pieces in a small box or in envelopes and code them to activities. When the child completes an activity he or she gets a personalized puzzle piece and deposits it in a separate envelope provided to collect that child's puzzle pieces. When all activities are done, the child has all the pieces to the puzzle and can work it. Make the puzzles of as many different kinds of transportation as possible, so that each child has a surprise picture.

A simple way to keep up with kids' work is to place a task board in the center. Make a poster paper chart of the activities to be completed and a list of children's names. Kids color in the appropriate box or put a star or gummed sticker beside activities completed. See the section in this chapter on How to Get Kids From Center to Center or Activity to Activity and the next chapter on Evaluation and Record Keeping for more ideas on this.

BE A WORD-EYE

CLUES I

1. Do two 👁v's from ▲.

2. Do five 👁v's from ◆.

3. Play a game from ●.

4. Take the posttest.

TASKBOARD

| Name | I | | | II | | | III | | | IV | | |
|------|---|---|---|---|---|---|---|---|---|---|---|---|
| | ▲ | ◆ | ● P | ▲ | ◆ | ● P | ▲ | ◆ | ● P | ▲ | ◆ | ● P |
| Ann | | | | | | | | | | | | |
| Bill | | | | | | | | | | | | |
| Ben | | | | | | | | | | | | |
| Chris | | | | | | | | | | | | |
| Clay | | | | | | | | | | | | |
| Carla | | | | | | | | | | | | |
| Eileen | | | | | | | | | | | | |
| Eddie | | | | | | | | | | | | |
| Frank | | | | | | | | | | | | |
| Gus | | | | | | | | | | | | |
| Hank | | | | | | | | | | | | |
| Lori | | | | | | | | | | | | |
| Larry | | | | | | | | | | | | |
| Leroy | | | | | | | | | | | | |
| Mary | | | | | | | | | | | | |
| Mark | | | | | | | | | | | | |
| Ned | | | | | | | | | | | | |
| Neil | | | | | | | | | | | | |
| John | | | | | | | | | | | | |
| Jack | | | | | | | | | | | | |

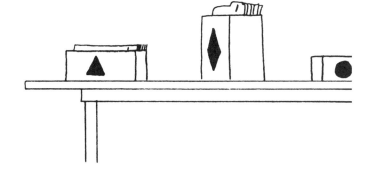

For a center such as one on creative arts activities, make a place in the room for children to hang up their creations. They can make or dictate sentence strips to explain each one or write directly on the finished work. You can also provide sheets of newsprint for kids to draw pictures or write explanations of the tasks as they finish them. Again, they can decorate and title them. For kids who don't read and write have an older child, assistant teacher, aide, or yourself take dictation for captions for their illustrations of the jobs they did.

A Halloween mask made by folding, cutting, and gluing paper.
Kathi D.

Adding Buttons

I counted the buttons. Then I added groups like this.
Jackie

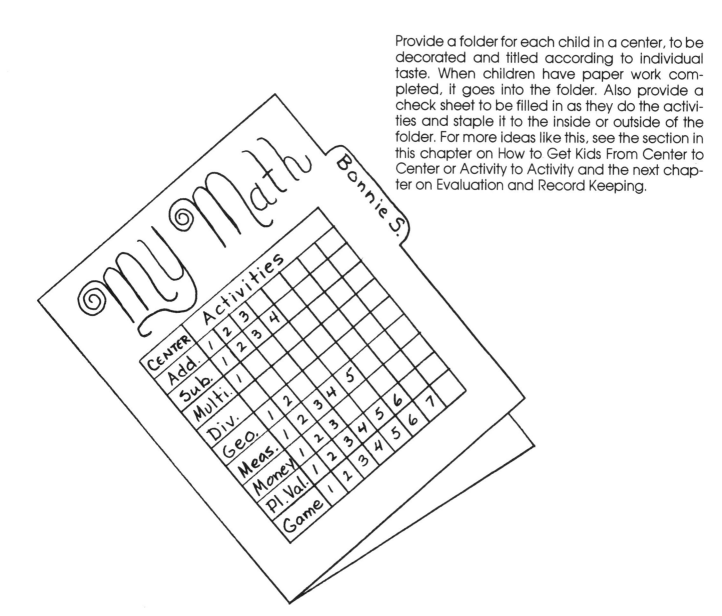

Provide a folder for each child in a center, to be decorated and titled according to individual taste. When children have paper work completed, it goes into the folder. Also provide a check sheet to be filled in as they do the activities and staple it to the inside or outside of the folder. For more ideas like this, see the section in this chapter on How to Get Kids From Center to Center or Activity to Activity and the next chapter on Evaluation and Record Keeping.

**HOW TO GET KIDS INTO CENTERS**

Whether you have your whole room set up in centers or you have only one or two going at a time, you need to introduce the center activities and directions and do a selling job on them. Make sure the kids know just what is in the center and what is expected of them. Explain and demonstrate the activities. Tell them how you will check them upon completion of the tasks. For example, say, "When you finish the math activity you will check your answers using the key taped to the filing cabinet near my desk, put the corrected paper in your math folder, turn your color square on the direction board to the blue side, then move on to your next activity or center." Exact directions from you will reinforce the written or pictorial directions you have placed in the center.

If there is no particular sequence in which the activities must be done, the kids are ready to choose their first place to work after you have completely explained all parts of the center.

"No sequence" means that they are free to do the activities in any order; however, they are still responsible for completing the work within the given time limit (a day, three days, a week).

HERE ARE 10 GAMES TO HELP YOU LEARN THE X FACTS.

YOU MAY PLAY THE GAMES IN ANY ORDER YOU WISH.

PLEASE DO ANY 6 OF THEM BY FRIDAY.

Thank

If there are particular centers for some kids or a certain order of activities kids are supposed to follow, you should discuss this. You might need to give out keys to certain centers or activities or point to a chart that is color coded to the activities. Kids would follow the color code; for example, red activity first, green second, and so on. Children must understand that they have to do the red activity before they can do the green because the activities are sequential. These techniques are especially good for your non-choosers and gatherers.

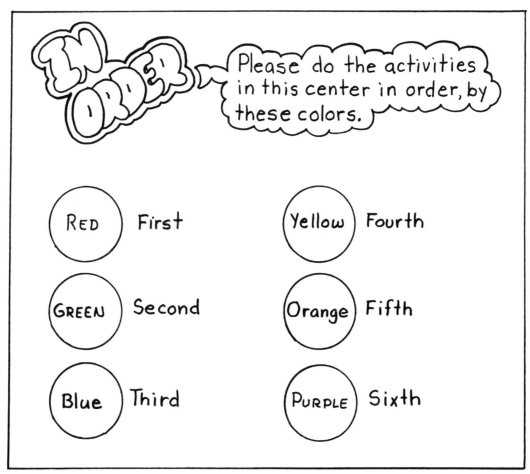

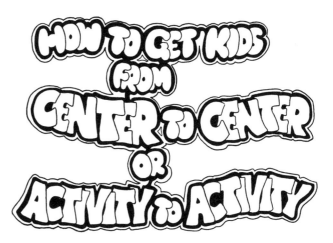

HOW TO GET KIDS FROM CENTER TO CENTER OR ACTIVITY TO ACTIVITY

When you introduce a center or centers, let kids work at them for a few days before you check up on who's done what. When you find non-finishers, get-losters, or flitterers, you can do some quick regrouping.

Make a mailbox for each child by nailing or-ange juice cans to a plywood board and plac-ing it on a table or the floor in a prominent place in the room. Other mailbox possibilities are shoe boxes or half-gallon milk cartons taped together and covered with contact paper; ice cream buckets nailed to a 2″ × 4″ stud and attached to the wall or stacked in a pyramid and taped together; and boxes with cardboard dividers. A good way to introduce mailboxes is to make them part of a learning center on the mailman (for primary grades) or the U.S. Postal Service (for elementary grades).

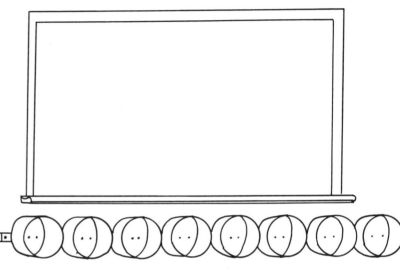

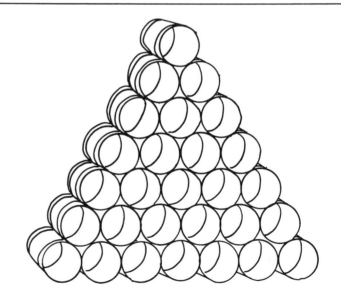

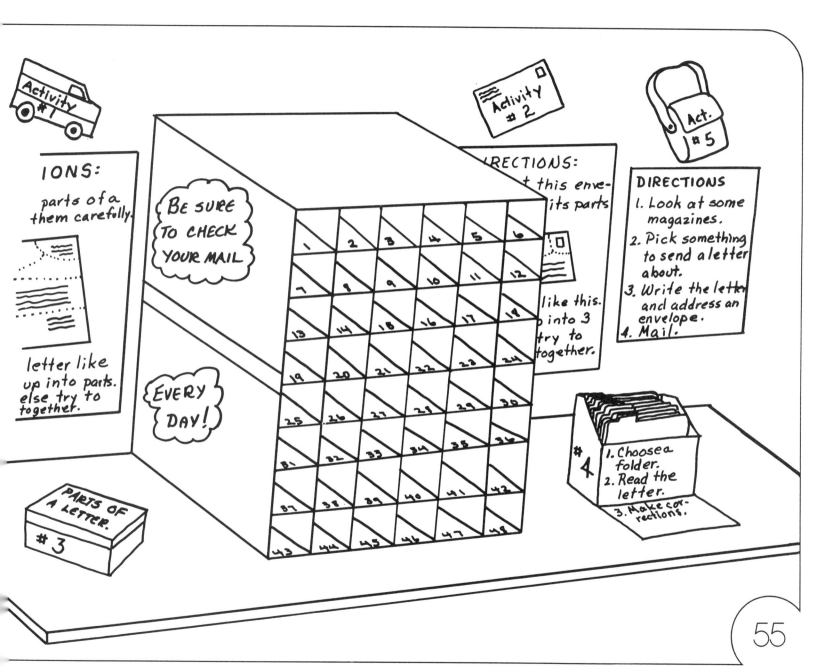

Send kids messages via letters or telegrams that give them positive reinforcement for good work or a gentle nudge toward improved on-task behavior. These messages can get children back on task and direct them toward the center or activities they should choose. They can then stay on course to finish their work in the time allotted. As kids read with more ease, substitute more and more words. Already-readers can help read telegrams if needed.

TEL-O-GRAM

Frank Smith

U R doing OK N the

1x2 center (stop) O π p

↑ the ☼ work (stop)

Mrs. Christi

## SMIL-O-GRAM

Judy A.

U did a ☀ job on 🏃 1 (stop) (GREEN) 2 the [cat] center and do 2 more 🏃 's (stop)

Mr. Kraft ☺

## SMIL-O-GRAM

Bill C.

U did ☀ work on UR 🥤 🏃. Try 1 more next 📅.

Ms. Allen ☺

The telegram idea can be used to assign centers for an entire day or week. If you have administered a pretest or in some other way have identified children with problem areas, a telegram can direct them to a specific skills center you wish them to complete.

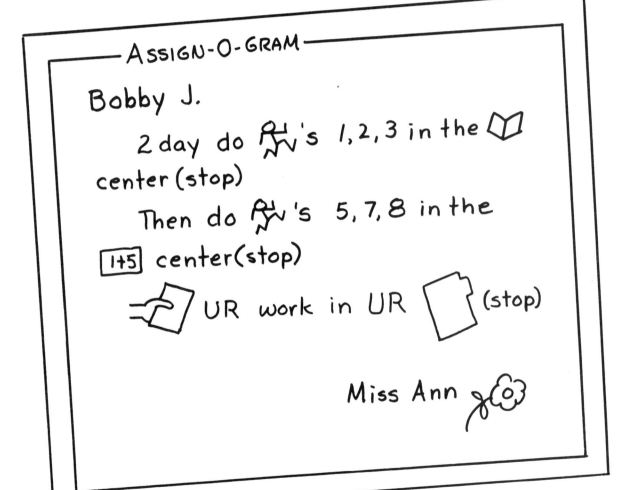

ASSIGN-O-GRAM

Bobby J.

2 day do 's 1, 2, 3 in the center (stop)

Then do 's 5, 7, 8 in the [1+5] center (stop)

UR work in UR (stop)

Miss Ann

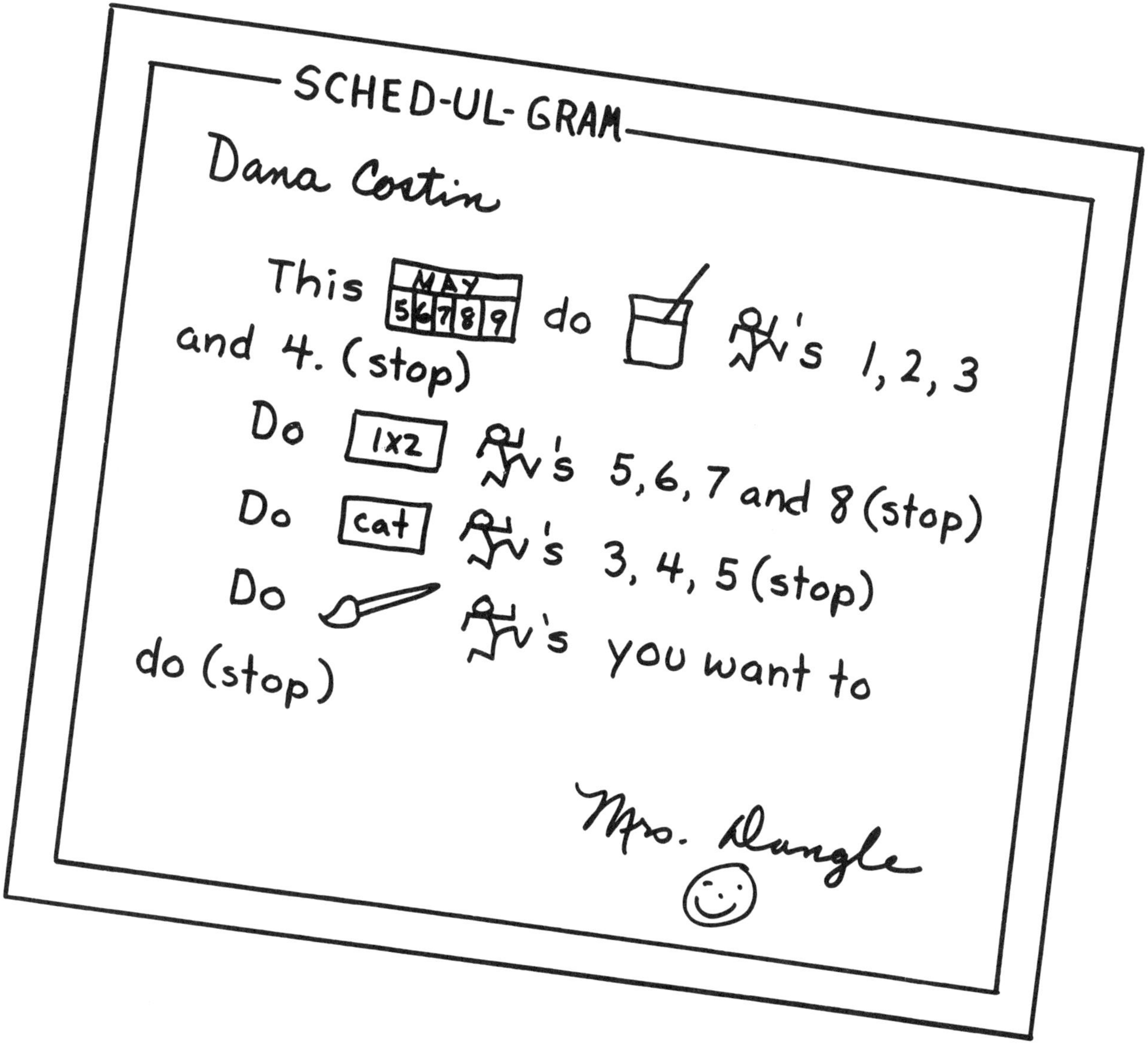

SCHED-UL-GRAM

Dana Costin

This [MAY 5 6 7 8 9] do 🥤 ⚆'s 1, 2, 3 and 4. (stop)

Do [1x2] ⚆'s 5, 6, 7 and 8 (stop)

Do [cat] ⚆'s 3, 4, 5 (stop)

Do 🖌 ⚆'s you want to do (stop)

Mrs. Dangle ☺

59

When planning, either with kids or by yourself, for what centers and what sequence of work should be done for a day or week, use other devices besides the mailbox to stamp your efforts with success. A dittoed form, to be filled out for or by each child as a plan of action for the day or week, is one option.

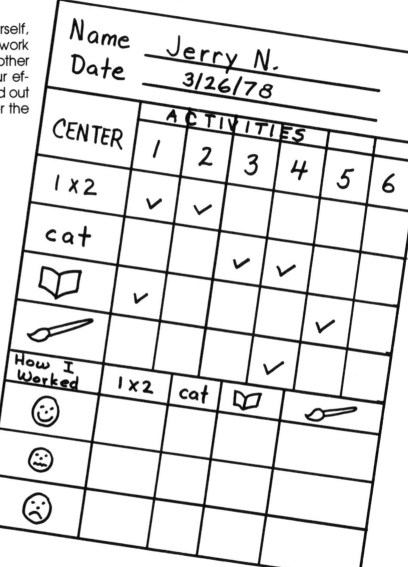

| Name | Jerry N. | | | | | |
| --- | --- | --- | --- | --- | --- | --- |
| Date | 3/26/78 | | | | | |

| CENTER | ACTIVITIES | | | | | |
| --- | --- | --- | --- | --- | --- | --- |
|  | 1 | 2 | 3 | 4 | 5 | 6 |
| 1 x 2 | ✓ | ✓ |  |  |  |  |
| cat |  |  | ✓ | ✓ |  |  |
| 📖 | ✓ |  |  |  |  |  |
| 🖌 |  |  |  |  | ✓ |  |
| How I Worked |  |  |  | ✓ |  |  |
|  | 1 x 2 | cat | 📖 |  | 🖌 |  |
| ☺ |  |  |  |  |  |  |
| 😐 |  |  |  |  |  |  |
| ☹ |  |  |  |  |  |  |

60

| | M | T | W | TH | F |
|---|---|---|---|---|---|
| **Name** Carl T. | | | | | |
| **Dates** 3/26/78 TO 3/30/78 | | | | | |
| CENTERS | M | T | W | TH | F |
| MATH | 1,2 | 3 | | 4 | 5 |
| SPELLING | A | B | C | D | E |
| READING | 4 | 5,6 | 7,8,9 | 10 | |
| SCIENCE | | | A | B | C | D |
| SOC. ST. | | | 7 | 8,9 | |
| | 5 | 6 | | | |
| SPORTS SPECIAL | Choose any three | | | | |
| HOW DID YOU WORK EACH DAY? | YEA | | | | |
| | EH? | | | | |
| | YUK | | | | |

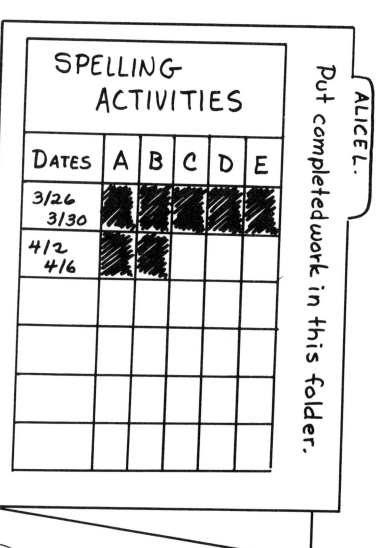

| SPELLING ACTIVITIES | | | | | |
|---|---|---|---|---|---|
| DATES | A | B | C | D | E |
| 3/26 3/30 | ■ | ■ | ■ | ■ | ■ |
| 4/2 4/6 | ■ | ■ | | | |
| | | | | | |
| | | | | | |
| | | | | | |
| | | | | | |
| | | | | | |

ALICE L.

Put completed work in this folder.

Whether it is a daily or weekly plan, this form can be placed in a folder, taped, or pinned up in the center for the child to refer to. It can also be put in the child's mailbox or kept in a folder on your desk. The form should always be available for kids to use to check off their progress. As they work through the activities, set up a conference or check-up time with them every few activities to see that they are on course. Build your check-up times into the form so that kids will know exactly when to find you and confer.

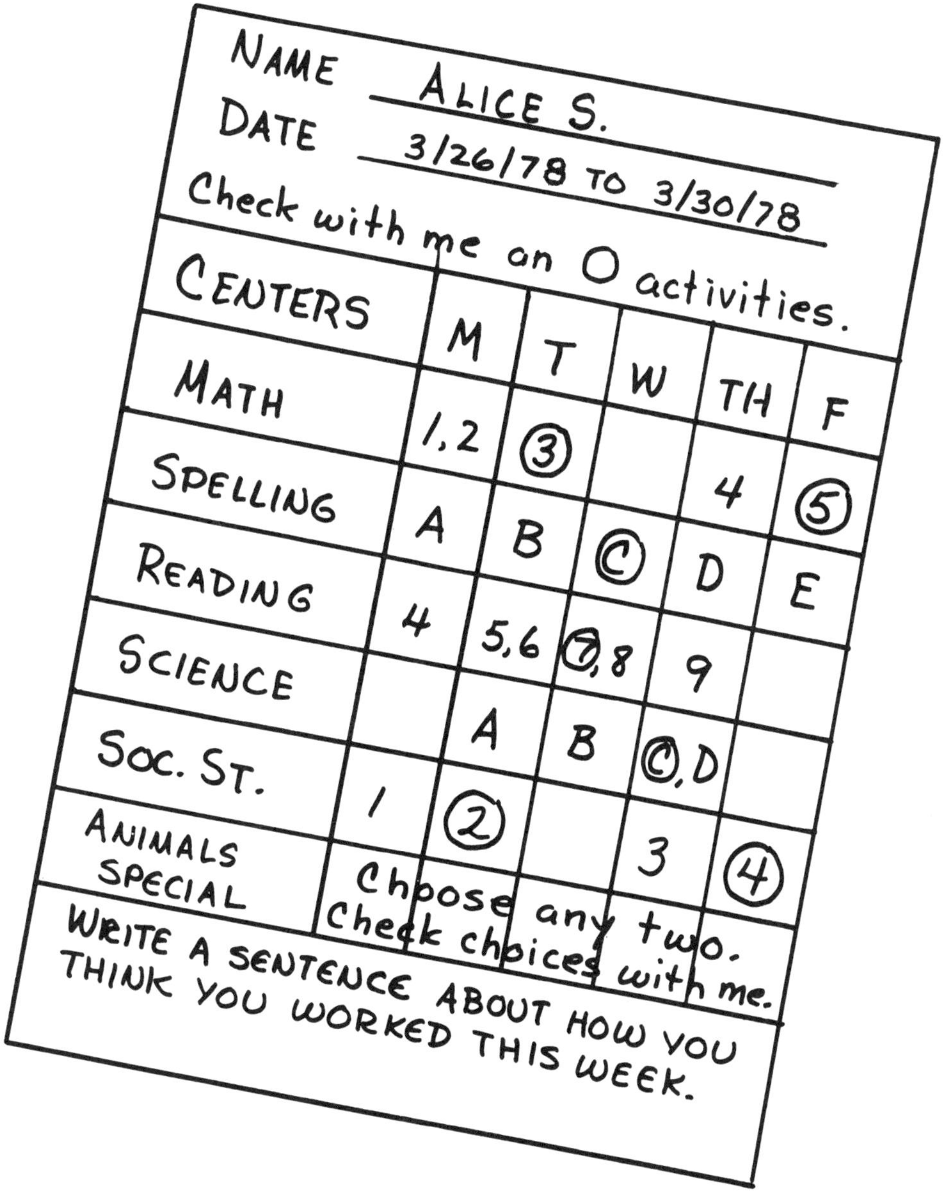

NAME ___ALICE S.___

DATE ___3/26/78 TO 3/30/78___

Check with me on O activities.

| CENTERS | M | T | W | TH | F |
|---|---|---|---|---|---|
| MATH | 1,2 | ③ | | 4 | ⑤ |
| SPELLING | A | B | ©️ | D | E |
| READING | 4 | 5,6 | ⑦,8 | 9 | |
| SCIENCE | | A | B | ©️,D | |
| SOC. ST. | 1 | ② | | 3 | ④ |
| ANIMALS SPECIAL | Choose any two. Check choices with me. | | | | |

WRITE A SENTENCE ABOUT HOW YOU THINK YOU WORKED THIS WEEK.

Another idea for getting kids from center to center is to issue a set of "shuttle" tickets that are color coded to the centers or to the activities in a center. Give each center a color. For example, the math center is blue, the science center is red, the reading center is green, the creative arts center is yellow, and the social studies center is purple. Each child receives five construction paper tickets, each ticket being one of the five colors. On the blue ticket list all the math activities for the week in the order that they should be done (if there is a sequence). After children finish an activity they get their tickets punched beside that activity, place their work

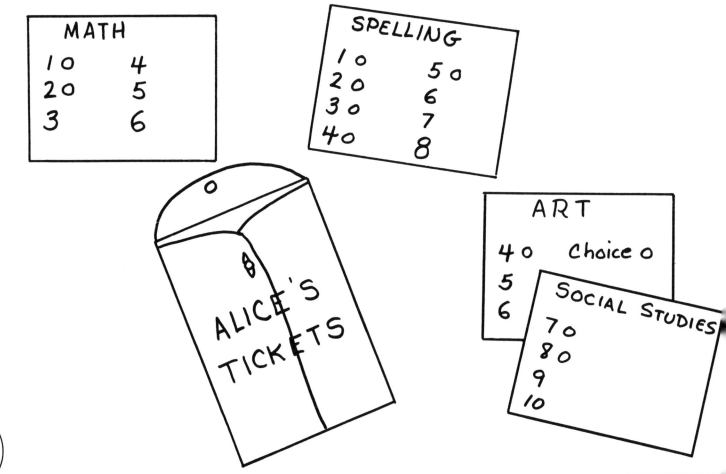

(if it is paper work) in folders provided in the center, and check their names off on your master list beside the activity completed. They do the same for each color-coded ticket for each list of activities until, at the end of the week, each ticket is completely punched for each center. You can check up on who's done what and at what intervals by looking at the set of tickets. Children can wear the envelopes containing tickets around their necks during the day, pin them to a bulletin board, or keep them in their mailboxes.

Use a manila folder or envelope in each center to collect work. Your master list can be a dittoed sheet stapled to the front of this folder or envelope, or it can be a poster paper chart hung in the center. The master list should list all the kids' names down the left-hand column and all activities in the center across the top. Either the children or you should check off completed tasks during the week. This informs kids which jobs they have done and which ones they still need to complete.

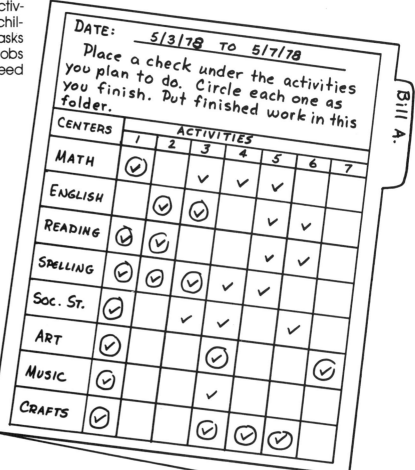

DATE: 5/3/78 TO 5/7/78

Place a check under the activities you plan to do. Circle each one as you finish. Put finished work in this folder.

Bill A.

| CENTERS | ACTIVITIES | | | | | | |
|---------|---|---|---|---|---|---|---|
| | 1 | 2 | 3 | 4 | 5 | 6 | 7 |
| MATH | ✓ | | ✓ | ✓ | ✓ | | |
| ENGLISH | | ✓ | ✓ | | ✓ | ✓ | |
| READING | ✓ | ✓ | | | ✓ | ✓ | |
| SPELLING | ✓ | ✓ | ✓ | ✓ | ✓ | | |
| SOC. ST. | ✓ | | ✓ | ✓ | | ✓ | |
| ART | ✓ | | | ✓ | | | ✓ |
| MUSIC | ✓ | | | ✓ | | | |
| CRAFTS | ✓ | | | ✓ | ✓ | ✓ | |

# MATH CENTER RECORD

✓ Started
Ⓥ Finished

## ACTIVITIES

| NAMES | 1 | 2 | 3 | 4 | 5 | 6 | 7 | 8 | 9 | 10 |
|-------|---|---|---|---|---|---|---|---|---|----|
| Susan | | | | | | | | | | |
| Alice | | | | | | | | | | |
| James | | | | | | | | | | |
| Karen | | | | | | | | | | |
| Sandy | | | | | | | | | | |
| Judy D. | | | | | | | | | | |
| Kathi | | | | | | | | | | |
| Bonnie | | | | | | | | | | |
| Judy S. | | | | | | | | | | |
| Mel | | | | | | | | | | |
| Craig | | | | | | | | | | |
| Jackie | | | | | | | | | | |
| Ruth | | | | | | | | | | |
| Sam | | | | | | | | | | |

Set up a treasure hunt that will take kids from center to center in a certain order. Make a map of the room with a directed path to the "treasure." The map should be accompanied by directions.

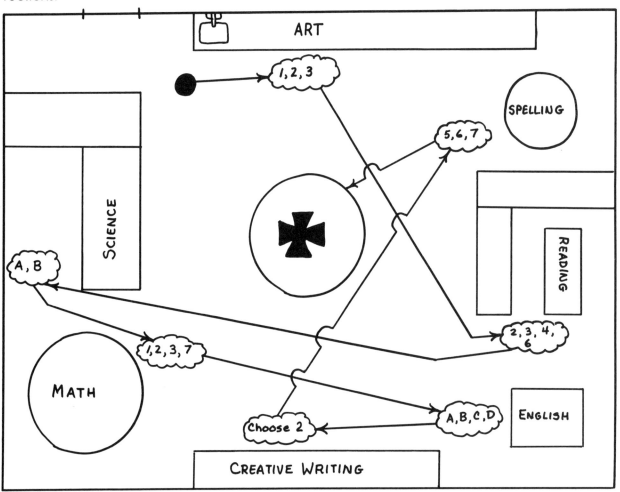

The kids work along through the day or week until they reach the end, and the treasure, which can be a fun activity or privilege. Be a guide and facilitator to keep kids on "hunt" in their quest for the treasure. Each child's map or group of children's maps should be somewhat different to ensure that they will not all be at the same center at the same time.

Many kids can make most of these plans and choices themselves, and almost **every** child can learn. They can plan the week's activities and choices and post their plan in the room or leave it in their mailboxes. Check to be sure they have included all the activities they need. This planning takes some time but it also prevents disorganization. The children will feel secure in knowing which direction to head in, and the increase in their ability to be responsible for their own learning is a welcome dividend. Remember that one of the hidden outcomes of working in learning centers is self-directed learning.

## TREASURE HUNT

Start at ●

ART ~ Hang pictures before going on to the next center.

READING ~ Be extra quiet!

SCIENCE ~ Put your experiment record in your folder.

MATH ~ Did you show all your work?

ENGLISH ~ Be sure to leave your ticket.

CREATIVE WRITING ~ Check with me before going on to the next center.

SPELLING ~ There is a "special" task here. Be sure you do it!!!

 ~ KEEP THE TREASURE A SECRET!!!

# HOW TO KEEP THINGS IN ORDER IN CENTERS

You will experiment — and probably have experimented — with room arrangements to see what way suits your purposes best. We have included some possible arrangements in our illustrations to start you thinking about all the different kinds of spaces you can offer children in a room. Enough space to do activities and projects, quiet spaces, noisy spaces, and orderly spaces are a few components of a good room arrangement. We have also included a room arrangement grid and a furniture template in the Appendix at the back of this book for you to use in planning the layout of your room **before** you move all the heavy furniture around over and over again.

## ROOM ARRANGEMENT KEY

### FURNITURE

C - CABINET
CB - CHALKBOARD
CD - CARDBOARD DIVIDER
DS - DISPLAY STAND
F - FILE

R - RUG
S - SHELVES
SD - STUDENT DESK
T - TABLE
RT - ROUND TABLE

TD - TEACHER DESK

### ROOM A

1. CONFERENCE AREA
2. RECORD KEEPING AREA
3. CREATIVE WRITING CENTER
4. HANDWRITING CENTER
5. SPELLING CENTER
6. ART CENTER
7. BOOK/READING CENTER
8. DIRECTED TEACHING AREA
9. MATH CENTER
10. SOCIAL STUDIES/SCIENCE CENTER

### ROOM B

1. TEACHER/CONFERENCE AREA
2. BOOK/READING AREA
3. SPELLING/ENGLISH CENTER
4. HANDWRITING/CREATIVE WRITING CENTER
5. SOCIAL STUDIES CENTER
6. MATH AREA/CENTER
7. DIRECTED TEACHING AREA
8. ARTS/CRAFTS AREA

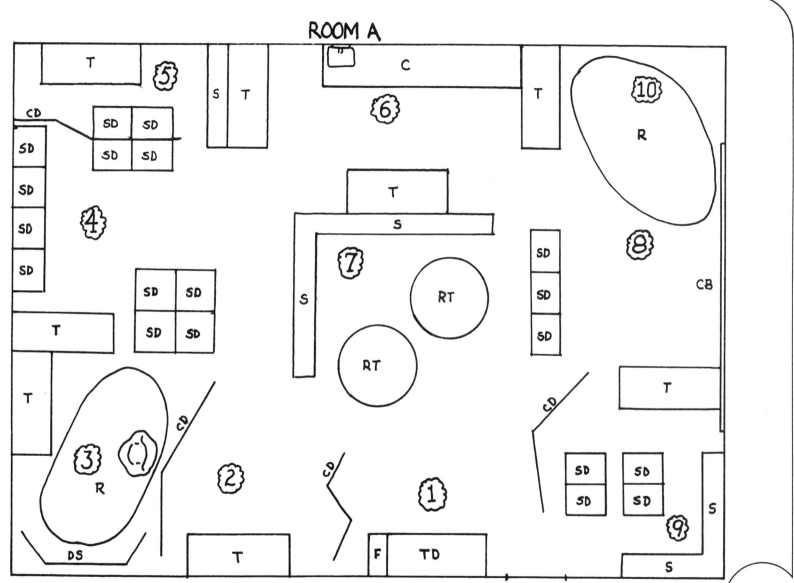

ROOM A

71

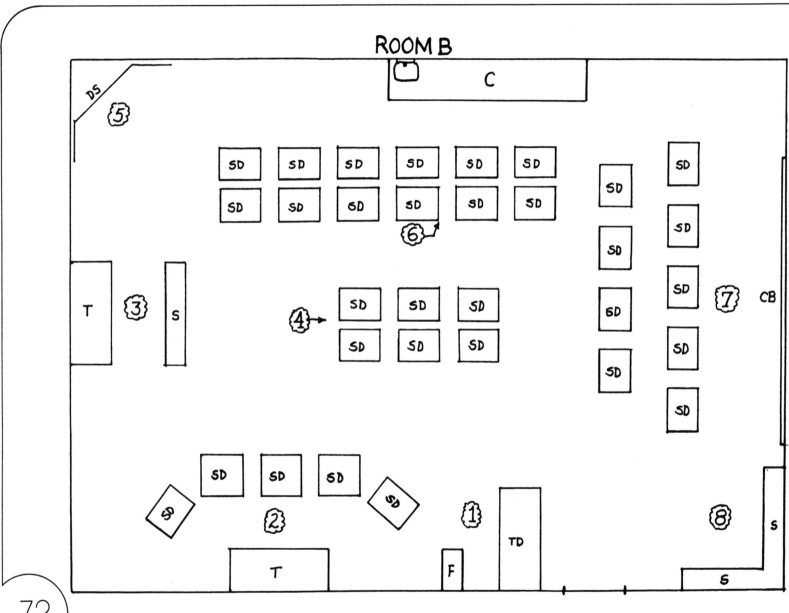

ROOM B

Plan rules for centers with the children. Keep these at a minimum. Kids will make more rules than necessary, so guide them in making only those rules really needed, or let them go ahead and proliferate rules, then discuss which ones can be eliminated.

## CENTER RULES

1. TALK SOFTLY.

2. STAY WITH THE ACTIVITY UNTIL IT IS DONE.

3. PUT THE ACTIVITY BACK INTO ITS BOX OR BAG WHEN DONE.

4. PUT THE BOX OR BAG ON ITS SHELF OR TABLE WHEN DONE.

5. ASK A FRIEND IF YOU NEED HELP, BUT DO YOUR OWN WORK WHEN YOU CAN.

6. USE THINGS IN THE CENTER GENTLY.

7. CLEAN UP WHEN YOU ARE DONE.

8. BE SURE TO FOLLOW ALL DIRECTIONS.

Show children how you have constructed activities. Some have many pieces, but they also have a box or plastic bag to hold them. The box or bag has a number, color, or other symbol on the outside, and each piece has that same symbol on its back. This system aids students in getting the right pieces back into the correct receptacle.

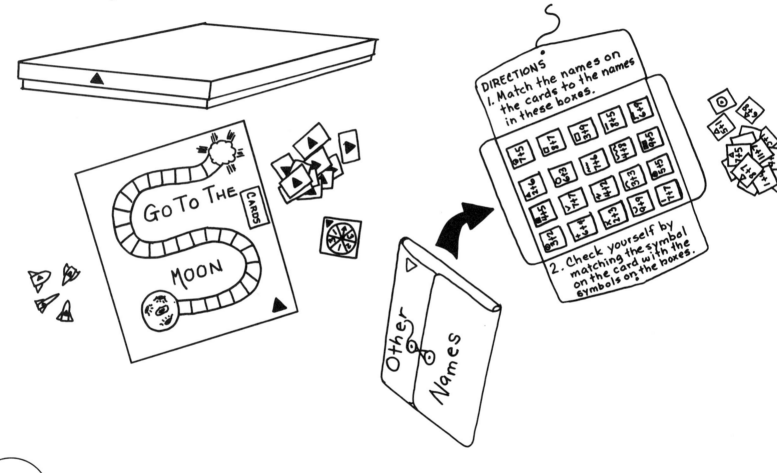

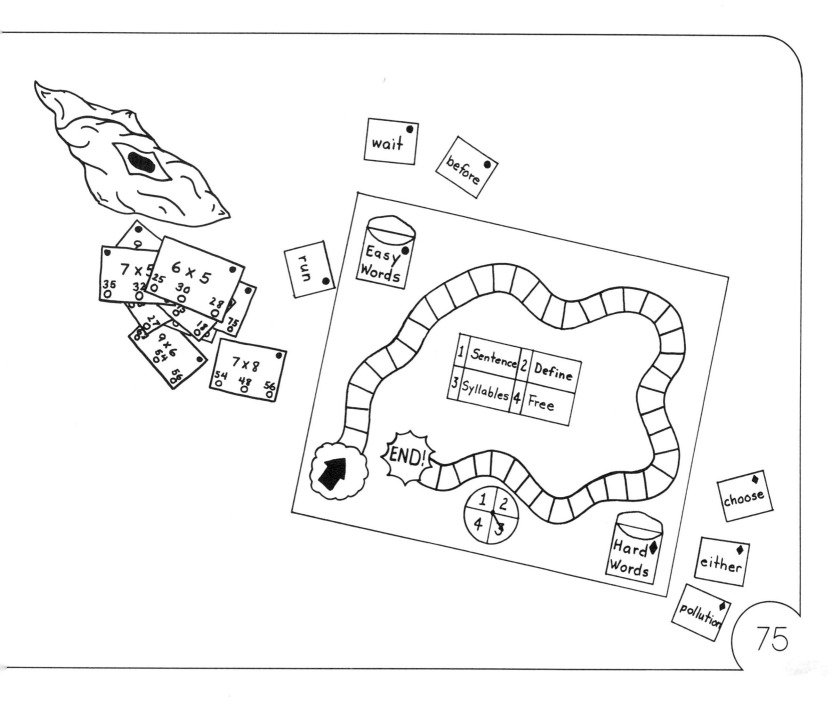

Each activity should also have a place on a shelf or table, or in a box. This place is also coded by number, color, or symbol for kids' convenience. Emphasize that they must cooperate in getting the pieces in the right box or bag and in getting the box or bag back in its correct place on the shelf or other activity holder so that the next user can find it.

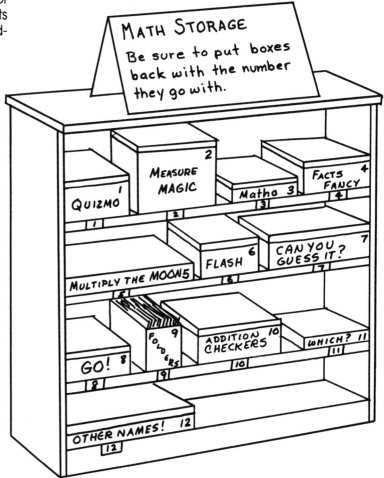

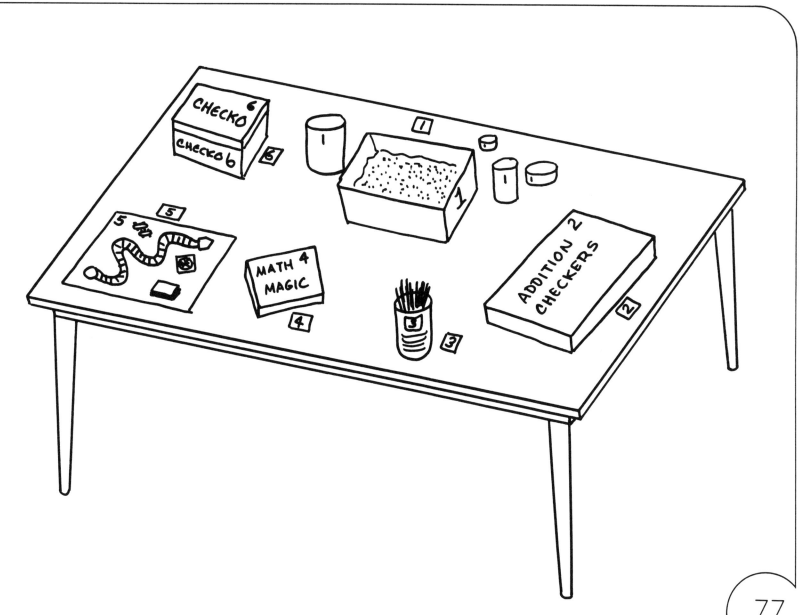

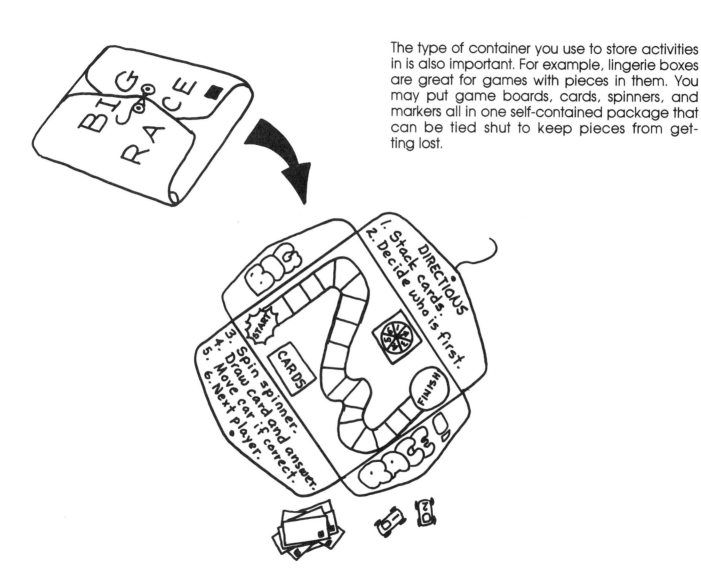

The type of container you use to store activities in is also important. For example, lingerie boxes are great for games with pieces in them. You may put game boards, cards, spinners, and markers all in one self-contained package that can be tied shut to keep pieces from getting lost.

BIG RACE

DIRECTIONS
1. Stack cards.
2. Decide who is first.
3. Spin spinner.
4. Draw card and answer.
5. Move car if correct.
6. Next player.

START

CARDS

SPIN

FINISH

# 5. EVALUATION AND RECORD-KEEPING

Determining what children are doing and how well they are doing in center activities is a difficult and complicated task. There is no way to get around this fact: evaluation and record keeping involve a great deal of time, carefully organized effort, and much concern for detail. And you must not fritter away the foregoing on the value-judgment process of comparing each child's performance to the performance of other children. Your energies should be directed toward evaluating what we consider the two main objectives of what a child does in centers: (1) progress (is he or she getting better at the task?), and (2) responsibility (is he or she developing a sense of knowing what to do, when to do it, and how to do it?). We feel, particularly in evaluating not-yet readers, that evaluation based on anything else is a sop to please teachers, parents, and administration, not an honest effort to determine whether or not kids are learning.

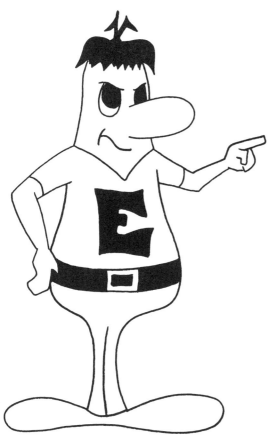

To serve the purposes we feel it should serve for not-yet readers (and any other kids for that matter), evaluation must concentrate on the formative potential of all learning for each child — scholastic growth in skills, concepts, and generalizations in the various content areas that make up the usual school curriculum, and personal growth as a learner in self-direction and responsibility/freedom (see chapter 1, Hidden Outcomes). Both **what** children are learning and **how** they are learning to function as learners are of equal importance to any evaluation you make.

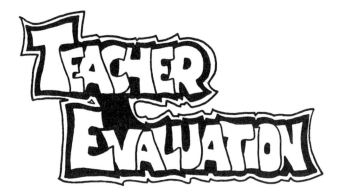

# TEACHER EVALUATION

Taming this two-headed beast, evaluation, calls for double-edged tactics. First, the procedures you use must focus on all the elements of growth achievement (growth in skills, concepts, and generalizations), self-direction (growth in the ability to stay on task, complete short- and/or long-range projects, and make plans for one's work), and responsibility/freedom (growth in the ability to accept learning tasks, carry through with plans, not interfere with the work of others, and assist others when needed). Second, these procedures must involve the child in the process of evaluating his or her own growth. The teacher's evaluation task is both to analyze the child's learning and the child as a learner and to instruct the child in self-evaluation.

If you, the teacher, can accept this stance on evaluation, then nothing remains but to take up your sword. No one form is better than another for this type of evaluation. Any checklist can be utilized to record observations of children's functioning as learners as long as it is planned to measure formative growth in achievement, self-direction, and responsibility/freedom. (For record-keeping ideas, see Keeping Track of Progress, the section that follows.)

You might wish to try this form in periodic evaluation conferences with kids and/or parents as a way to report growth. Feel free to alter it to fit your curriculum. Each person — you, the child, and the parents, if the parents are or become involved enough in your program to be able to do it — is asked to complete a copy of the form. A check mark indicates how the person views the child's progress in achievement (A), self-direction (SD), and responsibility/freedom (R/F) in each of the content areas. Then everyone (teacher-child-parent or teacher-child) sits down together, compares evaluations (any records or samples of work should be there for use), and discusses any differences in evaluation that occur (and some will occur!). The key to this activity is that, over a period of time, the discussion and resolution of differences demonstrate to children what evaluation means and how they should evaluate themselves. Repeated use of this approach will awaken children to how much control they have over both **what** they learn and **how** they learn.

NAME _____ LEVEL _____ DATE _____

| MATH | A | SD | R/F | READING | A | SD | R/F | SPELLING | A | SD | R/F |
|---|---|---|---|---|---|---|---|---|---|---|---|
| Outstanding | | | | Outstanding | | | | Outstanding | | | |
| Above Average | | | | Above Average | | | | Above Average | | | |
| Average | | | | Average | | | | Average | | | |
| Below Average | | | | Below Average | | | | Below Average | | | |
| ENGLISH | A | SD | R/F | Soc. STUDIES | A | SD | R/F | SCIENCE | A | SD | R/F |
| Outstanding | | | | Outstanding | | | | Outstanding | | | |
| Above Average | | | | Above Average | | | | Above Average | | | |
| Average | | | | Average | | | | Average | | | |
| Below Average | | | | Below Average | | | | Below Average | | | |

TEACHER COMMENTS:

CHILD COMMENTS:

TEACHER PLANS:

CHILD PLANS:

_____ TEACHER    _____ CHILD

**SELF-EVALUATION THROUGH SELF-CHECKING**

An instant-involvement technique for making children enthusiastic about self-evaluation is the use of self-checking devices in learning center activities and games. This technique also helps you with your split-personality problem of being in five places at one time! We know what you're thinking now. You're thinking that if the answers are there on an answer key or anywhere the kids can see them, they will **cheat**.

Let us interject a thought or two about cheating. Why do kids cheat? Is it because they are all basically dishonest? We don't think so. We think that kids cheat because our educational system has been geared toward "getting the right answers." If what they are being asked to do is too difficult for them, the only way to get the answer is to look — at an answer sheet or at someone else's work. We suggest that you encourage kids to recognize that errors and "not knowing" are everyday occurrences for most people. "Not knowing" is only an indication of what they still need to learn and what they **can** learn. And that realization means growth. We also suggest that if activities are too difficult, you may have misjudged a child's ability (teachers make mistakes, too!) and may need to adjust the task to the child's needs. Finally, you communicate a message of trust, very subtle but no less effective, to children when you encourage them to check themselves. Try some of the following ideas and see if the kids you work with don't live up to your most optimistic expectations.

Make up a set of cards with questions in the content areas of math, science, social studies, and language arts on the front and answers on the back. Write the questions and answers upside down in relation to each other. When students put a question into the top slot of the magic computer, the answer will come out the bottom slot. The kids must say the answer before the computer spews it out. You can call this activity Challenge the Computer.

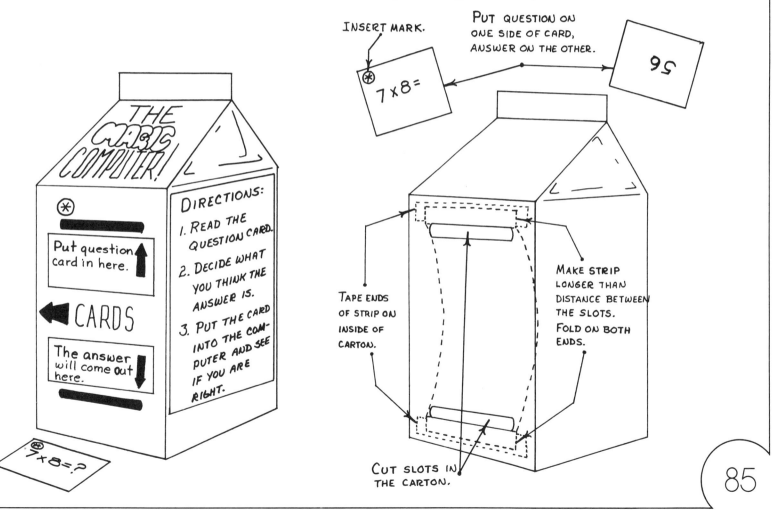

INSERT MARK.

PUT QUESTION ON ONE SIDE OF CARD, ANSWER ON THE OTHER.

7 x 8 =

56

THE MAGIC COMPUTER!

Put question card in here.

CARDS

The answer will come out here.

DIRECTIONS:
1. READ THE QUESTION CARD.
2. DECIDE WHAT YOU THINK THE ANSWER IS.
3. PUT THE CARD INTO THE COMPUTER AND SEE IF YOU ARE RIGHT.

7 x 8 = ?

TAPE ENDS OF STRIP ON INSIDE OF CARTON.

MAKE STRIP LONGER THAN DISTANCE BETWEEN THE SLOTS. FOLD ON BOTH ENDS.

CUT SLOTS IN THE CARTON.

Many tasks can be divided into puzzle pieces. For example, a math activity called How Many? can be drawn on poster paper rectangles (or any other shape) and cut apart into a two-piece puzzle. Children know they have chosen the right answer if their puzzle pieces fit together. Three- and four-piece puzzles give the kids a greater challenge.

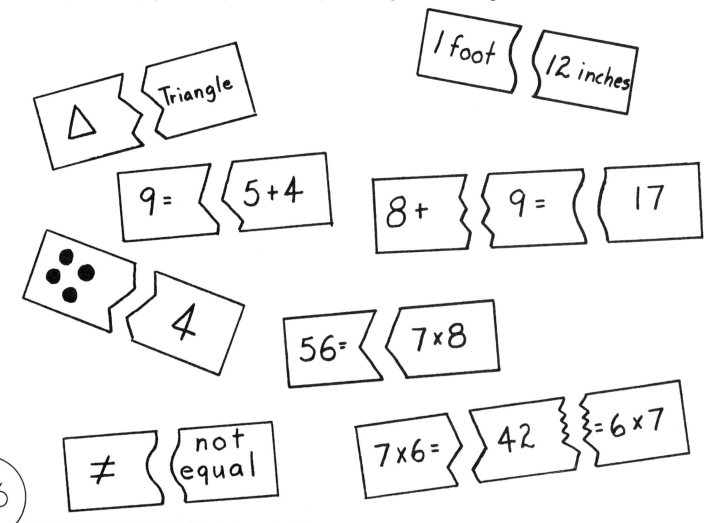

Math is not the only subject that you can puzzle up! Put antonyms or rhyming words on puzzle pieces. Have kids match baby animals to their parent animals for a puzzler. How about states and their capitals, rivers and their continents, countries and their continents, words and their definitions? Why don't **you** puzzle some out?

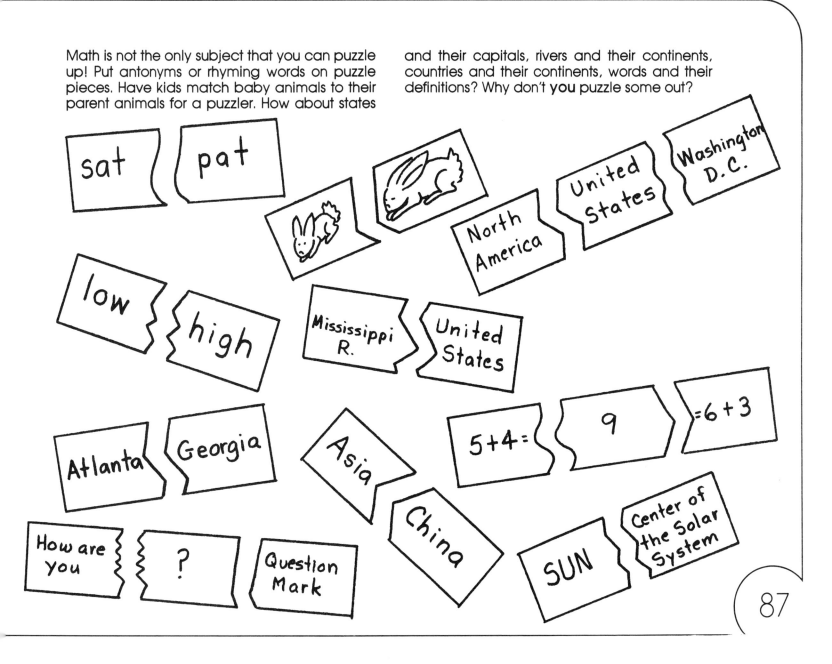

Sometimes kids will just work the puzzle instead of figuring out which answer goes with which problem, so sneak in a few puzzles cut alike. In order to check whether they have the right answer kids must first put the pieces together the way they think is correct, then turn the completed puzzle over. On the back you will have put symbols (numbers, words, shapes, or pictures) that will be complete if the responses are correct. Sneaky, aren't we?

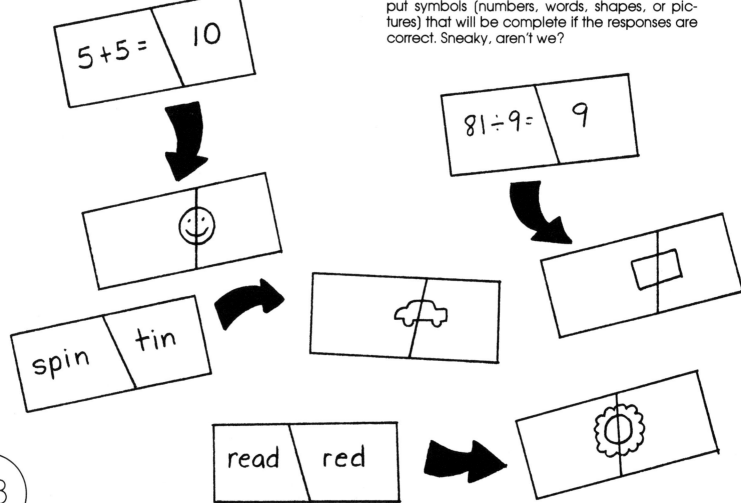

Another self-correcting activity is the old pencil-through-the-hole trick. Scatter problems on one side of a piece of poster paper, then punch a hole beside each problem. On the back, put the answer next to the hole of the problem it belongs with. Children can check themselves alone or have friends work with them. The child says the answer while sticking a pencil through

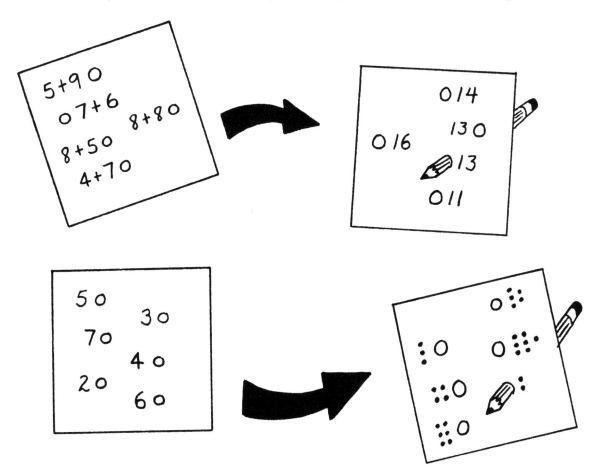

the hole. The child on the other side can see whether this is the correct response. Use color words and a swatch of color on the reverse side, number words with that number of dots or ob- jects on the opposite side, or do states and capitals using this method. The possibilities are almost limitless.

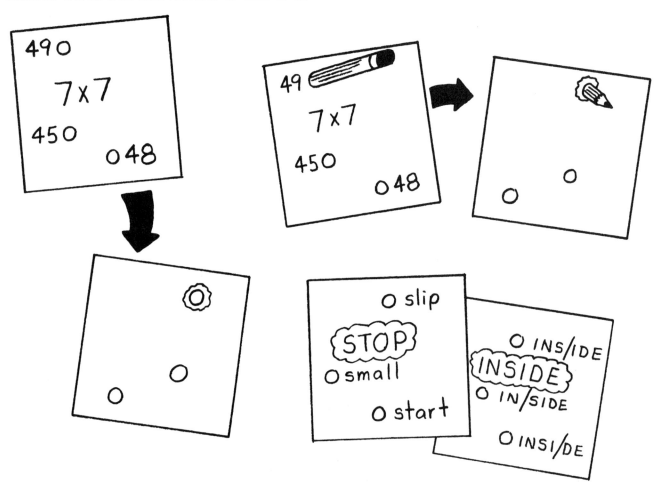

Some questions and answers are better placed on individual cards with possible answers listed over holes at the bottom. The student chooses the correct response, puts a pencil through the hole under it, then turns the card over to see whether it is the hole with a circle around it. This activity can be used with any subject area questions and answers.

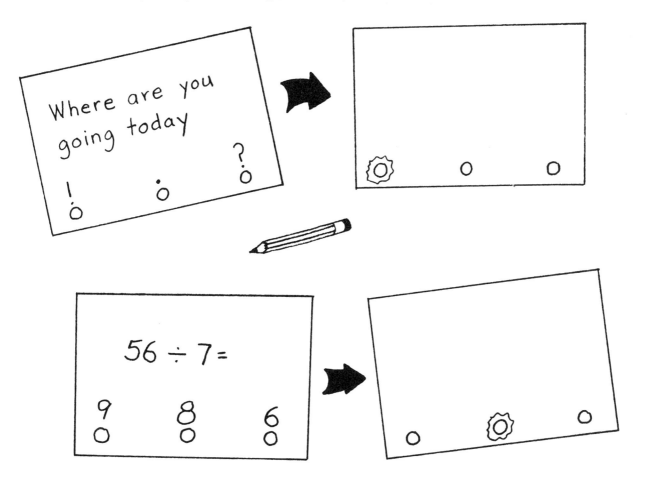

Yellow accent marker will not show through red or orange theme folder acetate. You can also get sheets of acetate in supply stores. So write problems in any color but yellow, then write the answer in yellow accent marker. Put the problem cards in a pocket whose front is of red or orange acetate. Students look at the top card, say the answer, pull the card out to check themselves, then do the next card showing until all the cards in the pocket have been pulled.

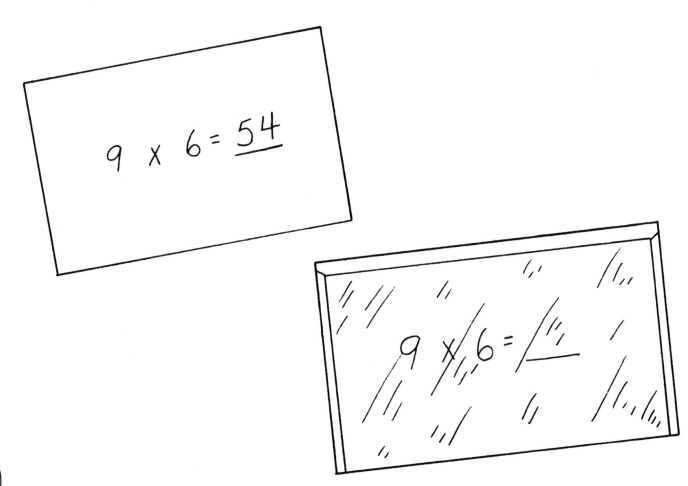

Another way kids can check their answers on the card back is to attach paper clips to the correct response(s) on the front, then turn the card over and look for a mark near the back of the paper clips they have attached.

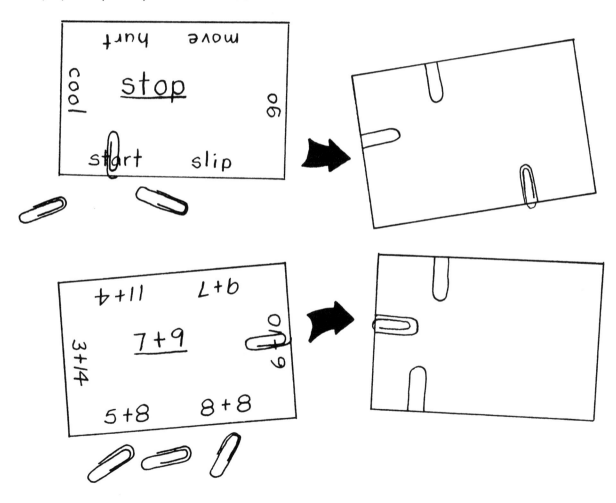

Make cards of problems with the correct responses out at the right edge of the page. Cover answers with the plastic spine from a theme folder. The student states the problem and answer, then slips the plastic down to uncover the correct answer and proceeds down the page, one problem at a time.

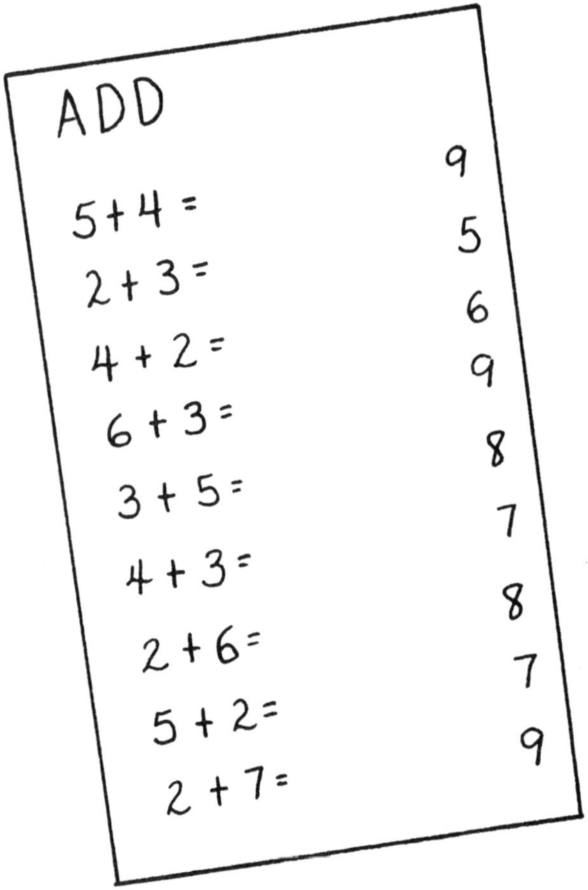

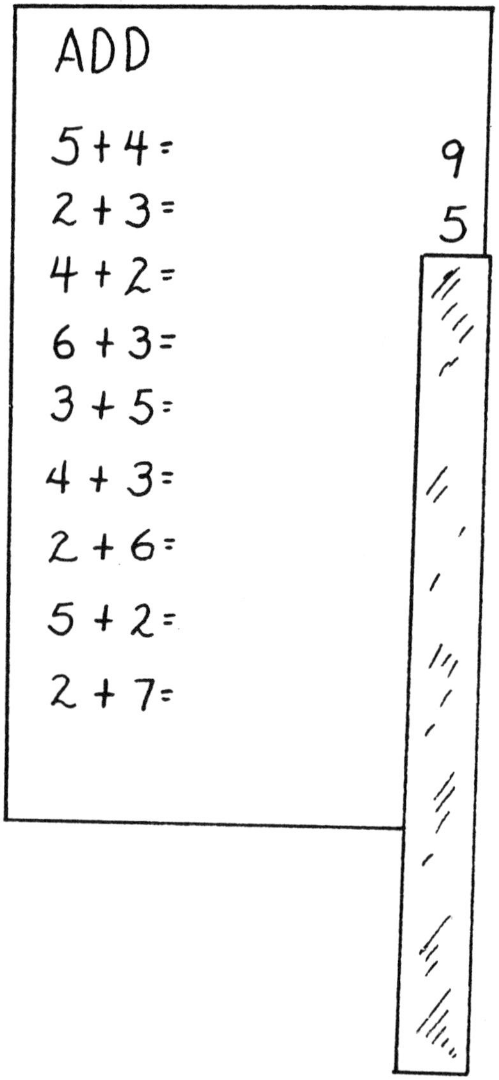

ADD

$5 + 4 =$      9

$2 + 3 =$      5

$4 + 2 =$      6

$6 + 3 =$      9

$3 + 5 =$      8

$4 + 3 =$      7

$2 + 6 =$      8

$5 + 2 =$      7

$2 + 7 =$      9

ADD

$5 + 4 =$      9

$2 + 3 =$      5

$4 + 2 =$

$6 + 3 =$

$3 + 5 =$

$4 + 3 =$

$2 + 6 =$

$5 + 2 =$

$2 + 7 =$

Prepare cards with a problem written in the middle in a certain color; for example, 5 × 7 might be written in red. Provide several possible answers with holes beside them. After the children choose their responses they check themselves by laying the question card over an answer key. The hole beside the correct answer,

35, will show red. By placing correct answers and holes in different locations on the cards you can use the different colors on the key for correct responses. Remember to write the problem in the same color that will appear in the hole beside the correct answer.

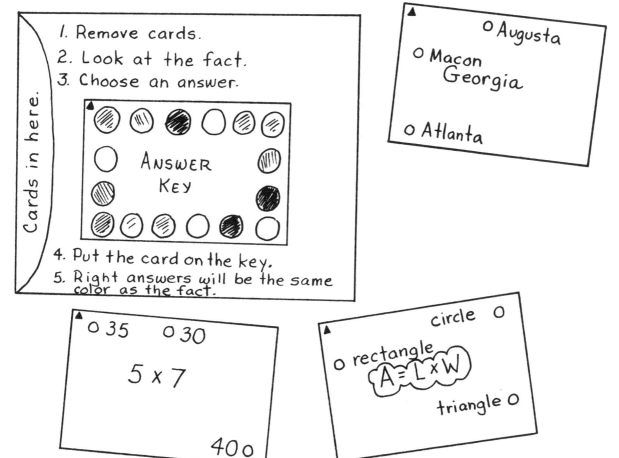

1. Remove cards.
2. Look at the fact.
3. Choose an answer.

ANSWER KEY

4. Put the card on the key.
5. Right answers will be the same color as the fact.

Cards in here.

o Augusta
o Macon
Georgia
o Atlanta

o 35    o 30

5 x 7

40 o

circle  o
o rectangle
A = L x W
triangle o

95

When possible, put the answers to an activity on the back of the card or object being used so that children can check themselves immediately. An example of this is an activity that requires children to match clothespins with numerals on them to a number of dots around a paper plate.

When children turn over the completed plate to check themselves, if an answer is correct the other side of the clothespin, which has a color painted on it, will match the color next to it on the paper plate.

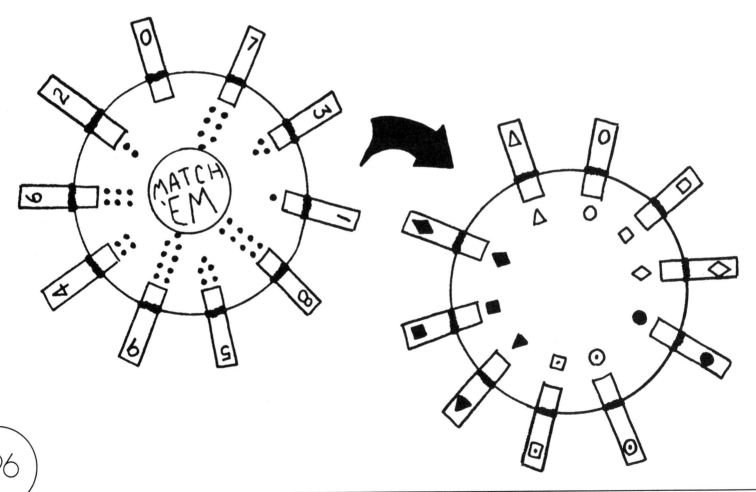

Another variation of the pencil-through-the-hole trick is the golf-tee-through-the-hole trick shown here. When all the answers are "teed," the pupil turns the wheel over to check. If the answers are correct, each golf tee will be in a hole with a circle around it. If incorrect responses appear, the student turns the wheel over, does the problem again, and rechecks it.

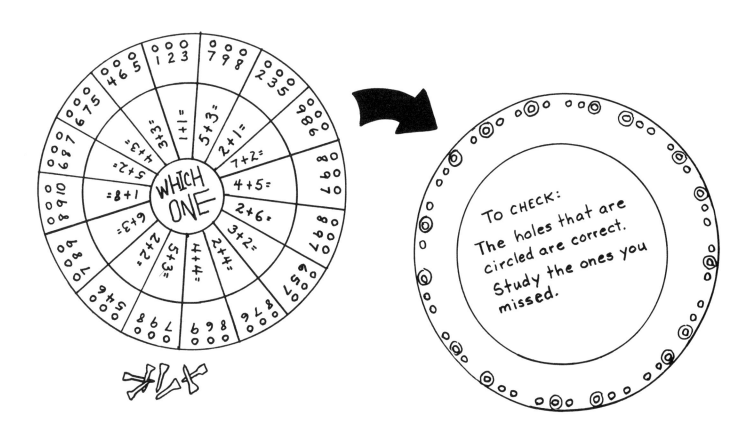

TO CHECK:
The holes that are circled are correct. Study the ones you missed.

Students will get a charge out of self-correcting with an electric answer board. Make an electric answer board by finding a sheet of pegboard (3' × 5'), brass fasteners, alligator clips, 20 feet of bell wire, a 9-volt dry cell, and a bell or buzzer or penlight bulb. Put all this together as shown. Set up matching-type activities on the board (addition problems and answers, states and capitals, vocabulary words and definitions, and so on). As the child matches two items correctly, the bell will ring or the buzzer will buzz or the light will light up.

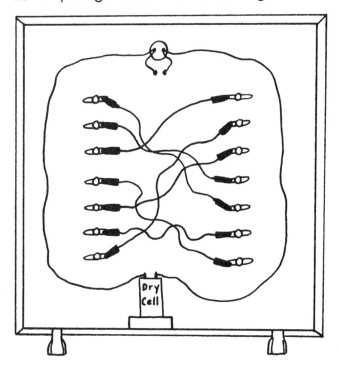

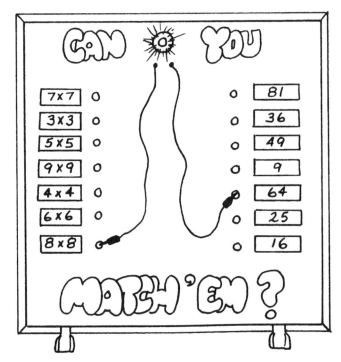

You can use an "undercover" device to present activities. A task that requires children to match color swatches to the words for the colors is a colorful example. Under the color word, which is put on the poster board with a brad, is a swatch of the color. After having matched up the whole board, the child peeks under each color word to verify all responses.

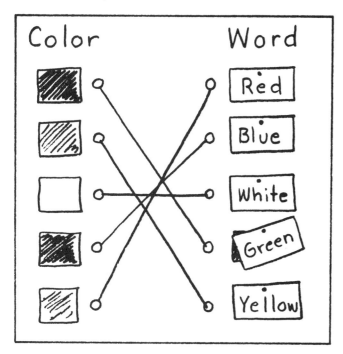

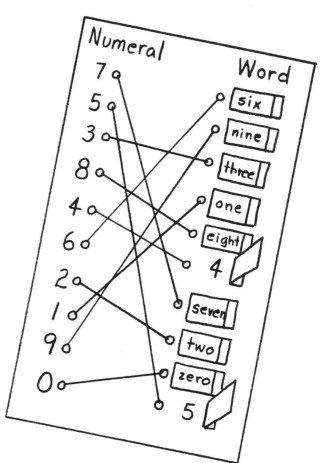

You cannot effectively evaluate children's growth without having something on which to base your decisions. That certain something is a record-keeping system by which you and the children can keep track of progress. Some guidelines for developing a record-keeping system are:

# Simple

1. **Keep records simple.** The more complicated record-keeping systems are, the more complicated and time-consuming will be the effort to keep them up to date and accurate and to use them. Children (and teachers, too!) rapidly lose interest in activities when they entail complicated records.

# NECESSARY

2. **Keep only necessary records.** No one likes to "clerk it" all the time. The only records necessary are those for keeping accurate, useful accounts of who needs to do what, who is doing what, and how well he or she is doing it.

3. **Be flexible and continually evaluate the records you keep.** As activities change, the children's needs change, your needs change, and the children become more responsible, be ready to change, revamp, or do away with unnecessary records. Maintain a steady monitoring of records. Ask children frequently how the record-keeping system is working and take their suggestions under consideration when the need for a change comes along.

PURPOSE

4. **Make sure records serve their intended purpose.** Some activities, such as projects and experiments, may require annotated records, while specific skills records may require a checklist for completed tasks. Some records may be class progress charts, while others may be individual charts kept in folders. Be sure your records will appropriately record the information you want them to contain.

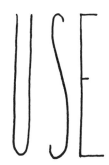

5. **Arrange your records for use.** Be sure your records are kept so that they are accessible to either an individual child or to the whole class in a particular area. Storing individual folders for children by curriculum areas might work best for you. A large three-ring binder might do the trick. The arrangement that **works best for you** is the one you should use.

**TEACHERS' RECORDS**

Here are some samples of records you might use to guide you in setting up your own system. These samples run the gamut from very general types on which you can record anecdotal comments to very specific types on which you can record skill mastery or activity completion. Which you use depends on what you need to be sure of to do an adequate job of evaluating the progress of your children.

| NAME _____ | | |
|---|---|---|
| DATE | ACTIVITY | OBSERVATION |
| O | | |
| O | | |
| O | | |
| | | |

| NAME: _____ |||||
|---|---|---|---|---|
| SKILL AREA: _____ |||||
| X MASTERED \ INITIATED R REINFORCED |||||
| O SKILL | DATE X | DATE \ | DATE R | COMMENTS |
|  |  |  |  |  |
|  |  |  |  |  |
| O |  |  |  |  |
|  |  |  |  |  |
|  |  |  |  |  |
| O |  |  |  |  |
|  |  |  |  |  |

NAME: _Bill Metly_

SKILL AREA: _Vocabulary_

X MASTERED    \ INITIATED    R REINFORCED

| O SKILL | DATE X | DATE \ | DATE R | COMMENTS |
|---|---|---|---|---|
| MEANINGS | 9/27 | | | On diagnostic test. |
| SYNONYMS | 10/3 | 9/29 | | Needs work on what synonyms are. 9/28 <br> Completed center activities very well. 10/4. |
| O ANTONYMS | | 10/6 | | Work with me in special group on this. 10/5 |
| HOMONYMS | | | | |
| ORIGINS | | | | |
| O NEW MEANINGS | | | | |
| SPECIAL VOCABULARY | | | | |

# DIAGNOSTIC RECORD FOR: _____

☒ MASTERED     ◺ INITIATED     ☐ NEEDS

| O NAMES | SKILL AREA: | | | | | | | | |
|---|---|---|---|---|---|---|---|---|---|
| | | | | | | | | | |
| | | | | | | | | | |
| | | | | | | | | | |
| | | | | | | | | | |
| | | | | | | | | | |
| | | | | | | | | | |
| | | | | | | | | | |
| | | | | | | | | | |
| | | | | | | | | | |
| | | | | | | | | | |
| | | | | | | | | | |
| | | | | | | | | | |
| | | | | | | | | | |
| | | | | | | | | | |
| | | | | | | | | | |
| | | | | | | | | | |
| | | | | | | | | | |
| | | | | | | | | | |
| | | | | | | | | | |
| | | | | | | | | | |
| | | | | | | | | | |
| | | | | | | | | | |
| | | | | | | | | | |
| | | | | | | | | | |
| | | | | | | | | | |

# DIAGNOSTIC RECORD FOR: __Math__

| ⊠ MASTERED | ⊠ INITIATED | ☐ NEEDS |
| --- | --- | --- |

## SKILL AREA: MULTIPLICATION SKILLS

| NAMES | Facts | Zero | Identity | Comm. | Assoc. | 2pl×1pl | 2pl×1pl | 3pl×1pl | 3pl×1pl |
| --- | --- | --- | --- | --- | --- | --- | --- | --- | --- |
| Fred | | | | | | | | | |
| Carolyn | | | | | | | | | |
| Susan | | | | | | | | | |
| Mary | | | | | | | | | |
| Rachel | | | | | | | | | |
| Paul | | | | | | | | | |
| Andrew | | | | | | | | | |
| Jack | | | | | | | | | |
| Priscilla | | | | | | | | | |
| Ellen | | | | | | | | | |
| Tom | | | | | | | | | |
| Roger | | | | | | | | | |
| Carol | | | | | | | | | |
| Mike | | | | | | | | | |
| Ann | | | | | | | | | |
| Chuck | | | | | | | | | |
| Matt | | | | | | | | | |
| Chris | | | | | | | | | |
| Peg | | | | | | | | | |
| Dan | | | | | | | | | |
| Phyllis | | | | | | | | | |
| Joann | | | | | | | | | |
| Karen | | | | | | | | | |
| Sally | | | | | | | | | |
| Mitch | | | | | | | | | |
| Kathy | | | | | | | | | |
| Allen | | | | | | | | | |

107

# DIAGNOSTIC RECORD FOR: READING

| ⊠ MASTERED | ⊠ INITIATED | ☐ NEEDS |
|---|---|---|

## SKILL AREA: VOCABULARY

| NAMES | Meanings | Synonyms | Antonyms | Homonyms | Origins | New Meanings | Special Vocabul. | | |
|---|---|---|---|---|---|---|---|---|---|
| Bill | | | | | | | | | |
| Chris | | | | | | | | | |
| Sherry | | | | | | | | | |
| Doug | | | | | | | | | |
| Louie | | | | | | | | | |
| Carl | | | | | | | | | |
| Marilyn | | | | | | | | | |
| Tom | | | | | | | | | |
| Kay | | | | | | | | | |
| Larry | | | | | | | | | |
| Sharm | | | | | | | | | |
| Bonnie | | | | | | | | | |
| Jackie | | | | | | | | | |
| Sam | | | | | | | | | |
| Terry | | | | | | | | | |
| Bernie | | | | | | | | | |
| Karen S. | | | | | | | | | |
| Mel | | | | | | | | | |
| Judy S. | | | | | | | | | |
| Kathi | | | | | | | | | |
| Craig | | | | | | | | | |
| Judy D. | | | | | | | | | |
| Dan | | | | | | | | | |
| Peggy | | | | | | | | | |
| Mike | | | | | | | | | |
| Karen L. | | | | | | | | | |
| Nancy | | | | | | | | | |
| Diane | | | | | | | | | |

# CENTER _____

| | √ Assigned | ⊘ Completed | ✗ Redo |

| NAMES | SKILL 1 ____ | | | SKILL 2 ____ | | | SKILL 3 ____ | | |
|---|---|---|---|---|---|---|---|---|---|
| | A● | B● | C● | A★ | B★ | C★ | A■ | B■ | C■ |
| | | | | | | | | | |
| | | | | | | | | | |
| | | | | | | | | | |
| | | | | | | | | | |
| | | | | | | | | | |
| | | | | | | | | | |
| | | | | | | | | | |
| | | | | | | | | | |
| | | | | | | | | | |
| | | | | | | | | | |
| | | | | | | | | | |
| | | | | | | | | | |
| | | | | | | | | | |
| | | | | | | | | | |
| | | | | | | | | | |
| | | | | | | | | | |
| | | | | | | | | | |
| | | | | | | | | | |
| | | | | | | | | | |
| | | | | | | | | | |
| | | | | | | | | | |
| | | | | | | | | | |
| | | | | | | | | | |
| | | | | | | | | | |
| | | | | | | | | | |
| | | | | | | | | | |
| | | | | | | | | | |
| | | | | | | | | | |

**KIDS' RECORDS**

These samples of kids' records will give you some ideas you might be able to adapt for your own students' use. Again, your choices will depend on what the purpose of the records is and how well they help the children keep track of their progress and learn the meaning of responsibility and self-direction.

# MY MATH RECORD

## NAME _____

| DATE | WHAT I DID |
|------|------------|
|      |            |
|      |            |
|      |            |
|      |            |
|      |            |
|      |            |
|      |            |

| THE READING RECORD OF _____ | | | |
| --- | --- | --- | --- |
| I'M READING | STARTED | COMMENTS | ENDED |
| O | | | |
| | | | |
| | | | |
| O | | | |
| | | | |
| | | | |
| O | | | |

# THIS WEEK IN MATH

Name _____

| DAYS | Center Activities Done | Pages in Book Completed |
|------|------------------------|-------------------------|
| MONDAY | | |
| TUESDAY | | |
| WEDNESDAY | | |
| THURSDAY | | |
| FRIDAY | | |
| | | |

# MATH RECORD

FOR _____

| SKILLS | MON | TUES | WED | THURS | FRI |
|--------|-----|------|-----|-------|-----|
|  |  |  |  |  |  |
| O |  |  |  |  |  |
|  |  |  |  |  |  |
|  |  |  |  |  |  |
|  |  |  |  |  |  |
|  |  |  |  |  |  |
| O |  |  |  |  |  |
|  |  |  |  |  |  |
|  |  |  |  |  |  |
|  |  |  |  |  |  |
|  |  |  |  |  |  |
| O |  |  |  |  |  |
|  |  |  |  |  |  |
|  |  |  |  |  |  |

# I AM READING ...

NAME _____

| TYPE | TITLE | SKILLS I'M WORKING ON | DATE |
|------|-------|----------------------|------|
| MYSTERY | | | |
| O | | | |
| | | | |
| SPORTS | | | |
| | | | |
| | | | |
| PEOPLE | | | |
| | | | |
| O | | | |
| SCIENCE | | | |
| FICTION | | | |
| | | | |
| ANIMAL | | | |
| | | | |
| | | | |
| SUBJECTS | | | |
| O | | | |
| | | | |
| OTHERS | | | |
| | | | |
| | | | |

# READ ON!

NAME: _____

| DAYS | PAGES I READ | WORKBOOK PAGES | GAMES PLAYED |
|------|--------------|----------------|--------------|
| MONDAY | | | |
| TUESDAY | | | |
| WEDNESDAY | | | |
| THURSDAY | | | |
| FRIDAY | | | |

# PROJECT PLAN

NAME _____ DATE _____

MY PROJECT IS ABOUT _____
_____

I USED THESE MATERIALS _____
_____

MY PROJECT REPORT WILL INCLUDE:

DISPLAY _____ SLIDES _____ PICTURES _____

FILM _____ CHARTS _____

I WILL BE READY TO REPORT ON _____

MY REPORT WILL TAKE _____ MINUTES.

I WILL NEED _____
_____

| EVALUATION OF: | PLAN | PROJECT REPORT |
|---|---|---|
| TEACHER | | |
| CHILD | | |
| PEER | | |

| | HOW I WORKED | MON. | TUES. | WED. | THURS. | FRI. | OVER-ALL |
|---|---|---|---|---|---|---|---|
| NAME _____ | | | | | | | |
| WEEK OF _____ | | | | | | | |

| | HOW I WORKED | MON. | TUES. | WED. | THURS. | FRI. | OVER-ALL |
|---|---|---|---|---|---|---|---|
| **MATH** | 🙂 | | | | | | |
| | 😕 | | | | | | |
| | 🙁 | | | | | | |
| **READING** | 🙂 | | | | | | |
| | 😕 | | | | | | |
| | 🙁 | | | | | | |
| **ENGLISH** | 🙂 | | | | | | |
| | 😕 | | | | | | |
| | 🙁 | | | | | | |
| **SOC. STUDIES** | 🙂 | | | | | | |
| | 😕 | | | | | | |
| | 🙁 | | | | | | |
| **SCIENCE** | 🙂 | | | | | | |
| | 😕 | | | | | | |
| | 🙁 | | | | | | |

Get out there, now. You have not yet begun
to fight!

| D | D | D | D | D | D | D | D | D | D | D | D | D |
|---|---|---|---|---|---|---|---|---|---|---|---|---|
| D | D | D | D | D | D | D | D | D | D | D | D | D |
| D | D | D | D | D | D | D | D | D | D | D | D | D |

| T | T | T | T | T | T | D | D |
|---|---|---|---|---|---|---|---|
| T | T | T | T | T | T | D | D |
| T | T | T | T | T | T | D | D |
| SC | SC | SC | SC | SC | SC | D | D |
| BC | BC | BC | BC | BC | BC | D | |

| TD | T | T | T | T | T | T |
|----|---|---|---|---|---|---|
|    | T | T | T | T | T | T |

PIANO

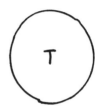

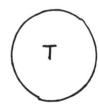

**KEY:**
- D – Student Desk
- T – Table
- TD – Teacher Desk
- SC – Storage Cabinet
- BC – Book Case

121

1 square = 1 foot

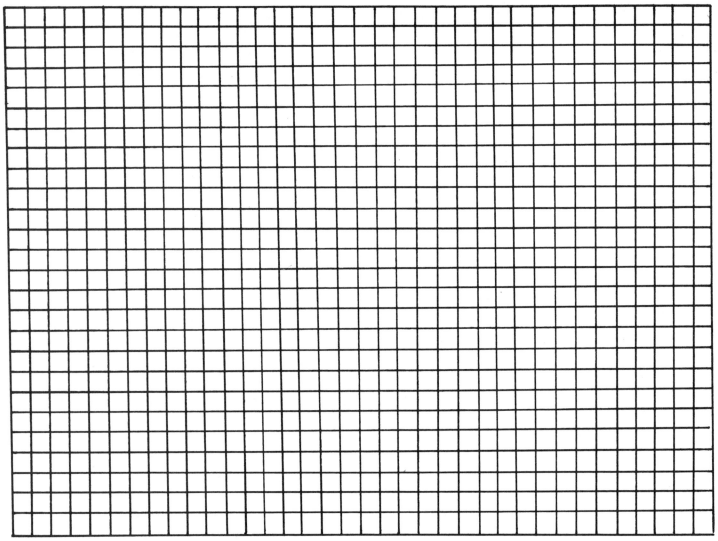